I.A.L.S. LIBRARY

All Right 1

A Refresher Course

von Michael Knight, David Whitling
und Per Jonason

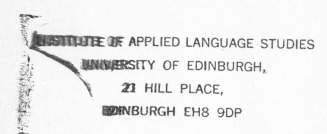

INSTITUTE OF APPLIED LANGUAGE STUDIES
UNIVERSITY OF EDINBURGH,
21 HILL PLACE,
EDINBURGH EH8 9DP

RECEIVED 20 FEB 1988

 Ernst Klett Stuttgart

D1437653

Inhalt

Vorwort

An den Kursteilnehmer

All Right ist für Kursteilnehmer gedacht, die bereits geringe Englischkenntnisse haben, aber nicht noch einmal bei Null anfangen wollen. Vor allem sollen Sie Gelegenheit erhalten, die englische Sprache einzuüben und zu **sprechen**.

Die einzelnen Arbeitsschritte mit *All Right* sehen folgendermaßen aus:

Situation	Strukturen	Übungen	Rollenspiel	Leseverständnis
Dialogue	**How to say it**	**Exercises**	**Role play**	**Read this**

Zuerst kommt ein **Dialogue** (Dialog), den Sie sich (vom Lehrer oder Tonträger) anhören, aber nicht in einem Durchgang lernen sollen. In erster Linie sollen Sie den Inhalt verstehen. Von den Dialogen gibt es zwei Versionen als Tonaufnahmen: eine „bereinigte", besonders deutlich gesprochene Version und eine „natürlichere", etwas schneller gesprochene Aufnahme mit Hintergrundgeräuschen. Die erste Version wird zu Beginn eingesetzt, um das Verstehen von Wörtern und Wendungen zu erleichtern. Mit der zweiten Version soll später Ihre Fähigkeit geschult werden, einer normalen, nicht aufbereiteten Unterhaltung zwischen englisch-sprechenden Personen folgen zu können.
Danach führen Sie mit der Seite **How to say it** (Wie man etwas sagt) sprachliche Übungen durch. Es handelt sich um Mini-Dialoge, die an den vorhergehenden Dialog anknüpfen. In *How to say it* arbeiten Sie mit einem Partner oder in einer Gruppe zusammen. Die Mini-Dialoge bestehen aus Äußerungen (meist Fragen und Antworten), mit denen Wortschatz, Grammatik und Aussprache geübt werden. Auf nachfolgende Übungen und auf die entsprechenden Grammatikabschnitte am Schluß des Buches wird verwiesen, z. B. bedeutet *Gr 8,* daß die Struktur in Abschnitt 8 des Grammatikanhangs behandelt wird. Wenn Sie die Beispielsätze und Erläuterungen in diesen kurzen Abschnitten zur Grammatik aufmerksam durchlesen, können Sie die wichtigsten in diesem Buch behandelten Strukturen kognitiv festigen. In den nun folgenden **Exercises** (Übungen) werden die gleichen Strukturen geübt wie in *How to say it.*

Ein Teil der Übungen ist schriftlich zu bearbeiten, damit sich der Lernstoff besser einprägt.
Jetzt sind Sie in der Lage, das **Role play** (Rollenspiel) zu bearbeiten. In diesem Spiel befinden Sie sich selbst in einer sprachlichen Situation, die stark an diejenige im ersten Dialog erinnert. Sie erhalten eine Rollenkarte, aus der hervorgeht, wer Sie sind und in welcher Situation Sie sich befinden. Ihre Aufgabe ist es, das Sprachmaterial anzuwenden, das in *How to say it* und in den *Exercises* geübt worden ist, doch nun in völlig freier Art und Weise. Wenn Sie wollen, können Sie beliebig improvisieren. Sollten Sie spüren, daß Sie sich im Rollenspiel bewähren, haben Sie das **Ziel** erreicht. Sie haben eine sprachliche Situation mit Ihren eigenen sprachlichen Mitteln bewältigt, und Sie werden sich in einer ähnlichen Situation in der Realität behaupten können.
Am Schluß jeder *Unit* befindet sich ein Lesetext **Read this**. Wie Sie wissen, muß man oft einem schweren Text bestimmte Informationen entnehmen können, einem Text, der sprachlich schwerer ist, als man selbst ihn sprechen oder schreiben könnte. Derartige Texte begegnen einem häufig in der Realität, z. B. beim Lesen eines Zeitungsartikels oder eines behördlichen Schreibens. In *Read this* werden Sie mit einem solchen Text konfrontiert, in dem Sie nicht jedes Wort zu verstehen brauchen, um ihm die wesentlichen Informationen entnehmen zu können.
In **Opinions** (Ansichten, Meinungen) werden schließlich Satzmuster angeboten, mit deren Hilfe Sie lernen können, Ihre eigene Meinung zu bestimmten Themen auf englisch auszudrücken.

The people in the book

Universal Services ist eine (imaginäre) internationale Firma, eine Art Dienstleistungsunternehmen, das alle Arten von Dienstleistungen anbietet. Es hilft beim Planen einer Reise, vermietet Autos, arrangiert Konferenzen, vermittelt Bekanntschaften usw. Man kümmert sich um ausländische Gäste, z. B. Geschäftsleute und Künstler. Das Hauptbüro von *Universal Services* ist in London, mit Zweigbüros in New York, San Francisco und Paris. Das Firmenmotto ist *„Your problem is our problem".*

Zum Personal des Londoner Büros gehört **John Austin,** Chefassistent und Mädchen für alles. Er ist ein netter und sympathischer, wenn auch etwas zerstreuter junger Mann, so um die 25. Bei seinen Kollegen ist er beliebt, obwohl er aufgrund seiner Zerstreutheit mitunter selbst in problematische Situationen gerät. Er ist Junggeselle und versucht ein bißchen, sich den Anschein eines Playboys zu geben.

Im Londoner Büro ist auch **Mary Hudson** angestellt. Ihr untersteht die Reiseabteilung. Mary arbeitet sehr gern mit John zusammen und ist manchmal wie eine Mutter oder große Schwester zu ihm.

Penny Lockwood ist Johns Freundin. Sie ist in einem anderen Unternehmen beschäftigt.

Dann ist da noch **Monique Simon,** ein französisches Mädchen. John lernte sie kennen, als sie vor zwei Jahren Aupair-Mädchen in England war. Als sie wieder nach London kommt, nimmt sie Kontakt mit John auf.

John Austin, 25,
Chefassistent
Universal Services

Mary Hudson, 46,
Reiseleiterin
Universal Services

Penny Lockwood, 26,
Ausbilderin
Minimax Ltd.

Monique Simon, 21,
Kindergärtnerin

1. Sorry I'm late!

Situation

Der Dialog dient zur Vorstellung der Situation sowie zur Einführung einer Reihe von nützlichen Wörtern und Wendungen. Hören Sie sich den Dialog mehrmals an, lesen Sie den Text durch und versuchen Sie, den Inhalt zu verstehen. Das Ziel besteht darin, die Situation und die Bedeutung der Sätze zu verstehen, bevor sie in *How to say it* geübt werden.

John Austin is at London Airport.
It is Monday morning.

John Oh, my God! It's after ten!
         Excuse me, are you Mr Petersen?

Man   No, I'm not.

John Oh, sorry.
         Excuse me, are you Mr Petersen?

Mr P Yes, that's right.

John I'm John Austin. I'm sorry I'm late.

Mr P That's all right.

Mrs P Oh, are you from Universal Services?
John That's right. I'm from the London office.
Mr P This is my wife, **Margret**.
John Hullo.
Mrs P Hullo.

John Here's a brochure – "What's On In London".
Mr P Thank you.
John And here's my card. Oh, sorry!
       That's my girl friend's photo. Here's my card.
Mrs P Thank you.
John Shall we go, then?
Mr P All right.

UNIVERSAL SERVICES
"Your problem is our problem".

John Austin
Assistant Manager
7 Baker Street, London. Tel. 01-908-3214

BETTER LATE THAN NEVER

(I'm) sorry [aɪm 'sɒrɪ] (es) tut mir leid
late [leɪt] (zu) spät
airport ['eəpɔːt] Flughafen
excuse me [ɪk'skjuːz mɪ] entschuldigen Sie
Universal Services [juːnɪ'vɜːsl 'sɜːvɪsɪz] Name einer
   Firma für allgemeine Dienstleistungen
office ['ɒfɪs] Büro
wife [waɪf] (Ehe-)Frau
What's on ['wɒts 'ɒn] Was ist los, was gibt es
card [kɑːd] Karte
assistant manager [ə'sɪstənt 'mænɪdʒə] Chefassistent

How to say it

Meeting and introducing people

Erläuterungen, Grammatik und Aussprache-cheübungen

Diese Seite soll dazu beitragen, die Sätze des Dialogs zu verstehen und den darin enthaltenen Grammatikstoff zu üben. Detailliertere Erklärungen finden sich in der Grammatik ab S. 126.

Die Sätze in den Kästen dienen dazu, die Grammatik und Aussprache zu üben. Üben Sie zunächst mit dem Kursleiter zusammen, danach mit einem Partner.

Hier wird also ein „Sprachtraining" durchgeführt, bevor die Sätze in den Übungen angewendet werden.

2

Are you	Mr Petersen? Mrs Petersen? Miss Newman? a nurse? Swedish? American? from London?	Yes, that's right. No, I'm not. I'm ..

● *Gr 1, 2, 22, 27B, 37* ● *Ex 2, 7*

Now make questions like this. Work in pairs.

1

I'm (I am)	John Austin.	Hullo.
	a secretary. an engineer. German. English. from London.	Are you?

● *Gr 1, 2, 22, 27C, 37* ● *Ex 6, 7*

Now make sentences like this about yourself. Work in pairs.

3

This is	my wife. my husband. Margaret. John.	Hullo.

● *Gr 22* ● *Ex 3, 7*

Now make sentences like this. Work in pairs.

Phrases

Practise saying these phrases.

Hullo.	Yes.	I'm sorry . . .
Excuse me.	No.	Thank you.
Sorry!	Yes, that's right.	Here's my card.
That's all right.	Oh, my God!	

(See Exercise 1.)

engineer [endʒɪˈnɪə] Ingenieur
nurse [nɜːs] Krankenschwester, -pfleger (in)
husband [ˈhʌzbənd] (Ehe-)Mann

Exercises

Mündliche und schriftliche Übungen
Hier wird die Anwendung nützlicher englischer Wörter und
Ausdrücke in Wort und Schrift geübt. Ein Teil läßt sich in der
Klasse zusammen mit dem Kursleiter oder mit einem Partner
durchführen, andere eignen sich für Hausaufgaben. So lernen
Sie, Wörter und Wendungen richtig anzuwenden, bevor Sie
zum freien mündlichen oder schriftlichen Gebrauch
übergehen.

One

Pairs

Put the sentences in A together with the right sentences in B.

A 1 Are you a secretary?
    2 I'm sorry I'm late.
    3 Excuse me, are you German?
    4 Hullo.
    5 Here's my card.

B 1 Hullo.
    2 That's all right.
    3 Thank you.
    4 No, I'm not.
    5 Yes, that's right.

Two

Are you John Roberts?

Write the questions and answers under the pictures.

1 *Woman* Excuse me, are you

....?

Man Yes, that's right.

2 *Woman* ....

....?

Man Yes, ...

3 *Man* ....

....?

Woman ....

4 *Man* ....

Julie Trent?

Woman No, I'm not.

5 *Boy* ....

....?

Girl No, ...

6 *Girl* ....

....?

Boy ....

Three

Introducing someone

In the picture one person is introducing another person.

1 *Mr Stevens* This is my wife.
  Wife Hullo.

2 *Mrs Crown* .... husband.
  Husband Hullo.

3 *Mrs Robinson* ....

  Husband ....

4 *Miss Black* ....

  Mother ....

5 *Mark* ....

  Father ....

6 *Ann* ....

  Charles ....

Role play

Rollenspiel

Das Rollenspiel bietet die Möglichkeit, das in den Dialogen und Übungen enthaltene englische Sprachmaterial in einer realistischen Situation anzuwenden. Gewöhnlich wird das Rollenspiel in Partnerarbeit durchgeführt. Hier verwenden Sie Ihr Englisch zur Kommunikation, zur Lösung von Problemen und zur Erlangung von Informationen.

You are at London Airport. Your teacher will give you more information.

Five

Landing Cards

The Petersens fill in Landing Cards at London Airport.

IMMIGRATION ACT 1971	LANDING CARD

Family name (in block letters) **PETERSEN**

Forenames **ALEX**   Occupation **DESIGN ENGINEER**

Date and place of birth **9.4.29 MUNICH, GERMANY**   Sex **MALE**

Nationality **GERMAN**   Signature **A. Petersen**

Full address in United Kingdom **CENTRE HOTEL, QUEENSWAY, LONDON W2**

NR	FOR OFFICIAL USE	V	BV	ST

Now you fill in your Landing Card.

IMMIGRATION ACT 1971	LANDING CARD

Family name (in block letters) ....

Forenames .... Occupation ....

Date and place of birth .... Sex ....

Nationality .... Signature ....

Full address in United Kingdom ....

NR	FOR OFFICIAL USE	V	BV	ST

block letters ['blɒk letəz] Druckbuchstaben, Versalien
occupation [ɒkjʊ'peɪʃn] Beruf
sex [seks] Geschlecht
male [meɪl] männlich
female ['fiːmeɪl] weiblich

United Kingdom [juːˈnaɪtɪd ˈkɪŋdəm] Vereinigtes Königreich (England, Schottland, Wales, Nordirland)

Six

Jobs

Write the questions and answers about these people's jobs.

typist ['taɪpɪst] Maschineschreiber(in), Typist(in)
shop assistant ['ʃɒp ə'sɪstənt] Verkäufer(in)
waiter ['weɪtə] Kellner
bank clerk ['bæŋk klɑːk] Bankangestellte(r)

Use these words.

a typist	a taxi driver
a bus driver	a cook
a housewife	*a secretary*
a shop assistant	a nurse
a policeman	a bank clerk
a business man	a student
a waiter	a traffic warden

For example:

Seven

Am, is, are

Fill in am ('m), is ('s) and are.

1 I .... Alex Petersen.

2 This .... my wife, Margret.

3 .... you British?

4 Yes, that .... right.

5 Here .... my passport.

6 I .... sorry I .... late.

7 That .... all right.

8 .... you a housewife?

9 No. I .... not. I .... a nurse.

10 This .... my husband.

11 .... you German?

12 Yes, that .... right.
  I .... from Stuttgart.

Eight

Translate these sentences

Translate these sentences into German.
Use idiomatic German.

1 Excuse me, are you Mr Smith?
2 I'm sorry I'm late.
3 This is my wife, Ingrid.
4 Here's my card.
5 Better late than never.

Now translate these sentences into English.
Try not to look at the sentences above!

6 Entschuldigen Sie, daß ich mich ver-
  spätet habe.
7 Hier ist mein Paß.
8 Besser zu spät als nie.
9 Verzeihung, sind Sie Frau Erdmann?
10 Das ist mein Mann, Götz.

Nine

Who has what job?

Read the information about the people. Then put the information together, so that you can say who has what job – like this:

Mr Reino Rantola is a Finnish waiter.

Peter is German. He is a teacher.
Miss Moen is from Norway.
Reino is a waiter. He is from Helsinki.
Mary is a nurse. She is English.
Allan is a shop assistant. He is from Stockholm.
Maria is Norwegian. She is a film star.
The German's surname is Grunder.
Mr Svanström is Swedish.
Mr Rantola is Finnish.
Mrs Dupont is a French housewife.
Mrs Falls is English.
Annette is a housewife.

> surname ['sɜːneɪm] Nach-, Familienname

London Airport

Lesen und verstehen

Mit diesen Texten wird die Fähigkeit geübt, einem schwereren Text Informationen zu entnehmen. Es handelt sich um Texte, wie man sie in Büchern, Prospekten und anderen gedruckten Materialien antrifft.

Hier brauchen Sie nur den Inhalt zu verstehen, so daß Sie daraus die wichtigsten Informationen entnehmen können. Es ist nicht nötig, daß Sie jedes einzelne Wort verstehen.

Answer these questions with Yes or No.
If you can't answer them, read the text and then try again.

1 Has London Airport — Heathrow got two passenger terminals for flights to Europe?
2 Do passengers with BA go to Terminal 2?
3 Do passengers with LH go to Terminal 2?
4 Must passengers check in at the airport 60 minutes before their Flight Departure?
5 Do coaches leave the Victoria Terminal 60 minutes before Flight Departure?
6 Can you bring into Britain 100 cigarettes from Germany?
7 Can you bring in two bottles of whisky from Germany?
8 Can you bring in two bottles of wine from Germany?

Heathrow

London Airport – Heathrow has two passenger terminals for passengers to and from Europe.
Terminal 1 is for passengers travelling with British Airways (BA).
Terminal 2 is for passengers travelling with all other airlines – e.g. Lufthansa, SAS, KLM etc.
GO TO THE RIGHT TERMINAL.
Passengers must check in at the right Terminal 30 minutes before Flight Departure.
Coaches leave the Victoria Terminal near Victoria Station every 15 or 20 minutes.
There are Tax-free shops at both Terminals for passengers leaving Britain.

Note: The Tax-free allowance *into* Britain from Germany is:
200 cigarettes *or* 8 ounces (250 grams) of tobacco.
One litre of spirits and two bottles of wine.

passenger ['pæsɪndʒə] Passagier, (Fahr-, Flug-)Gast
departure [dɪ'pɑːtʃə] Abflug, Abfahrt
coach [kəʊtʃ] (Flughafen-, Reise-)Bus
bring in [brɪŋ 'ɪn] einführen
travel with ['trævl wɪð] reisen, fliegen, fahren mit
allowance [ə'laʊəns] erlaubte Menge

In „Opinions" lernen Sie, Ihre Meinung zu einem Thema auf englisch auszudrücken.

Opinions

Why are you studying English?

Maria Berg, 47, taxi driver
"I need English for my work."

Anton Roman, 38, policeman
"I think English is fun."

Helene Karlsen, 29, nurse
"I want to go to England."

2. How are you?

John Austin takes Mr and Mrs Petersen to their hotel.
His friend David works at the Reception there.
It is Monday evening.

John Hullo, David. How are you?
David Fine, thanks. You?
John All right, thanks. Cold today, isn't it?
David Yes, horrible.

John This is Mr and Mrs Petersen.
David Ah, yes. Good evening.
Mr P Good evening.
Mrs P Good evening.
David Will you fill in this form, please.
 Your room is number twelve.
Mr P Thank you.

COLD TODAY, ISN'T IT?

David (to John) Well, how's your girl friend?

John Penny, you mean? She's all right, thanks.
Well, I must go now. See you on Wednesday.

David At the pub.

John Right. Cheerio.
Goodbye, Mr and Mrs Petersen.

Mr P Goodbye.

Mrs P Goodbye. Thank you for all your help.

John That's all right. Goodbye.

horrible ['hɒrəbl] furchtbar, schrecklich
fill in a form [fɪl 'ɪn ə 'fɔːm] ein Formular ausfüllen

How to say it

Greetings; asking for and giving information

1

How are	you?	Fine, thanks.
How's	your wife?	All right, thanks.
(is)	your husband?	
	Penny?	

• Gr 22 • Ex 3, 4

Now make questions like this. Work in pairs.

2

What's	your name,	please?	It's . . .
(is)	your address,		(It is)
	your telephone number,		
	your occupation,		I'm a . . .
	your nationality,		I'm . . .

• Gr 18, 20, 37

Now make questions like this. Work in pairs.
Don't forget to say please.

3

John Austin is	an assistant manager.	Is he?
He's (He is)	English.	
He isn't (He is not)	married.	Isn't he?
Mrs Petersen is	English.	Is she?
She's	married.	
She isn't	a doctor.	Isn't she?

• Gr 1, 2, 22, 27C, 37 • Ex 9

Now make sentences about other people. Work in pairs.

> **occupation** [ɒkjʊˈpeɪʃn] Beruf
> **married** [ˈmærɪd] verheiratet

4

It's	nice	today,	Yes, it is.
	nice and warm	isn't it?	
	cold		
	wet		
	windy		

• Gr 27 • Ex 2

Now make sentences like this.

Numbers

one 1 – two 2 – three 3 –
four 4 – five 5 – six 6 –
seven 7 – eight 8 – nine 9 –
ten 10 – eleven 11 – twelve 12

Days

Sunday Monday Tuesday
Wednesday Thursday Friday
Saturday   • Gr 38
today
morning afternoon evening

Phrases

Practise saying these phrases.

How are you?
Fine, thanks.
All right, thanks.

Thank you for all your help.
That's all right.
See you on . . .

Good evening.
Goodbye.
(See Ex 1.)

Exercises

One

Pairs

Put the sentences in A together with the right sentences in B.

A
1 Good evening.
2 Sorry I'm late.
3 I must go now.
4 See you on Monday at the pub.
5 How are you?

B
1 Goodbye.
2 Right.
3 That's all right.
4 Fine, thanks.

5 Good evening.

Two

The weather

Read this conversation.

A Nice today, isn't it?   *B* Yes, lovely.

Now read this conversation.

C Cold today, isn't it?   *D* Yes, horrible.

Now make other conversations about the weather with these words:

nice nice and warm nice and sunny	lovely wonderful beautiful	cold wet windy cloudy	horrible awful nasty

Three

The weather again

Read this conversation.

David Hullo, Mrs Smith. How are you?

Mrs S Fine, thanks. And you?

David All right, thanks. Wet today, isn't it?

Mrs S Yes, awful.

Now look at the picture and make a new conversation.

Pat Hullo, Mr Black. How ....?

Mr B ...., ...?

Pat All ...., ...

.... today, ...?

Mr B Yes, ...

Now make a conversation about the weather today.

Four

How's your wife?

Look at this example:

Alan *How's your wife?*

Mark *She's fine, thanks.*

John *How's your husband?*

Tina *He's fine, thanks.*

Now you write the conversations.

David .... your girl friend?

John ....

Sally .... your boy friend?

Penny ....

Susan .... Mr Crossman?

Jean ....

Pat .... Mrs Crossman?

Peter ....

Five

See you on Monday

Read this conversation.

Penny See you on Monday.

John Right.

Now make new conversations with the other days of the week:
Sunday, Tuesday, Wednesday, Thursday, Friday, Saturday.

Six

See you at the pub

Now read this conversation.

John See you at the pub.

Penny Right.

Now look at the pictures and words below and write the words under the right pictures.

the restaurant   the station   the airport
the match   the office   the party

1 ....

2 ....

Seven

On Monday at the pub

Now write five conversations like this, and read them with a friend.

Penny See you on Monday.
 John At the pub.
Penny Right.

Eight

Role play

You meet a friend in the street, have a conversation and arrange to meet again. Your teacher will give you more information.

3 ....

4 ....

5 ....

6 ....

Nine

He is at the bank

Look at these sentences. Write the right text under the pictures.

Albert is not at the post office.
It is not cold.
Mrs Petersen is not a doctor.
Mr Brown is not French.
The Swan is not a restaurant.
It is not Monday morning.

It is Saturday evening.
He is English.
It is a pub.
She is a nurse.
It is nice and sunny.
He is at the bank.

1 *Albert is not at the post office. He is at the bank.*

2 ....

3 ....

4 ....

5 ....

6 ....

Ten

Translate these sentences

Translate these sentences into German.
Use idiomatic German.

1 How are you?
2 Hot today, isn't it?
3 Ulla Berg isn't married.
4 I must go now.
5 What's your telephone number?

Now translate these sentences into English.
Try not to look at the sentences on the left.

6 Wie ist Ihre Adresse?
7 Wie geht's?
8 Kalt heute, nicht?
9 Alex Petersen ist verheiratet.
10 Wir müssen jetzt gehen.

Eleven

Who's who?

Mr and Mrs Blake are American.
Mr and Mrs Svensson are Swedish.
Mr and Mrs Dobson are English.

Who is Number 1?

It's Mr ....

Who is Number 2?

It's ....

Who is Number 3?

....

Who is Number 4?

It's Mrs ....

Who is Number 5?

....

Who is Number 6?

....

1

Who am I?

2

I'm not Mr Svensson.

3

My wife is English.

4

5

6

My pub

"London has over six thousand pubs, and I have one of them. Some of the pubs are very famous, like Dirty Dick's. Lots of tourists go there.

But most of them are like my pub, just ordinary places where ordinary people go for a drink with their friends.

I open at 10.30 in the morning and close at 2.30 in the afternoon. Then I open again at 5.30 and close for the day at 10.30 in the evening. We have funny opening times for pubs in England!

It's hard work, but I see lots of interesting people, and I like it. Cheers!"

Joe Hackett, the landlord of "The Rose and Crown".

Right or wrong?

Put "right" or "wrong" after the sentences.

1 Joe Hackett's pub is called Dirty Dick's.
2 Joe Hackett's pub is not an ordinary pub.
3 The pub opens at 10.30 in the morning.
4 It opens again at 10.30 in the evening.
5 It closes at 2.30 in the morning.
6 Joe likes his work.

> **famous** ['feɪməs] berühmt
> **ordinary** ['ɔːdnrɪ] gewöhnlich

Opinions

What's your favourite drink?

Elizabeth Silver, 42, secretary
"I like beer best."

Johnny Sands, 20, footballer
"I like milk best."

Anne Goodman, 56,
shop assistant
"I like a nice cup of coffee."

3. Shall we go out to

Alex and Margret Petersen are at their hotel in London.
It is Tuesday afternoon.

Margret Shall we go out tonight?
Alex Yes, good idea.
Margret Where's that brochure? From Universal Services.
Alex "What's On in London"?
Margret Yes.
Alex Here it is.
Margret Thanks. Ah! Would you like to go to Lady Jane's?
Alex What's Lady Jane's?
Margret "The best strip club in town".
Alex Oh Margret! No! I don't think so.
    What about a theatre?
Margret Yes, all right.
Alex I'd like to see a comedy. What's on?
Margret What about "The Man Who Could Do Every-
    thing"?
Alex Yes, good idea.

night?

How to say it

Making suggestions

1

Shall we	go out tonight? go to the theatre? go to a restaurant? go to a night club? go to a concert? have dinner at Black's Grill?	Yes, good idea. No.

• Gr 11, 32 • Ex 2

Make suggestions like this. Work in pairs.

2

Would you like to	go out tonight? go to the cinema? go to Lady Jane's? stay at home?	Yes. No, I don't think so.

• Gr 11, 35 • Ex 3

Make more suggestions like this. Work in pairs.

3

I'd like to (I would)	see a comedy. go to a concert. go to a strip club. go and have a drink.	Good idea! Well, *I'd* like to go to . . .

• Gr 35 • Ex 4

Say what you would like to do. Work in pairs.

4

What about	a comedy? a musical? a film? a jazz concert?	Yes, good idea. No, I don't think so.

• Gr 36

Make suggestions like this. Work in pairs.

5

What's	Lady Jane's? the Palladium? the Albert Hall? this?	It's a . . . (See page 34.)

• Gr 3, 36

Ask questions. Work in pairs.

Phrases

Practise saying
these phrases.

tonight
Here it is.
Good idea!
Yes, all right.
I don't think so.
(See Ex 1.)

the Albert Hall [ðɪ ˈælbət ˈhɔːl] Konzerthalle in London

Exercises

One

Pairs

Put the sentences in A together
with the right sentences in B.

A 1 Shall we go to the cinema tonight?
   2 Where's my passport?
   3 What about a strip club?
   4 Here's the brochure.
   5 Would you like to go to a Mozart concert?

B 1 Here it is.
   2 Thank you.
   3 Yes, good idea.
   4 No, I don't think so.
   5 Yes, all right.

Two

Shall we go to the cinema?

Robert would like to go to the cinema.
He says "Shall we go to the cinema?"

I.A.L.S. LIBRARY

Now you say, and then write the questions:

1 You would like to go to a night club.

....

2 You would like to go to the theatre.

....

3 You would like to go to a strip club.

....

4 You would like to go to a restaurant.

....

5 You would like to go to the cinema.

....

6 You would like to go to a pub.

....

7 You would like to go to a pop concert.

....

8 You would like to stay at home and watch
television.

....

....

> **watch television** [wɒtʃ ˈtelɪvɪʒn] fernsehen

Three

Fill in the missing words

Peter wants to go out with Susan,
but she isn't very interested.
She says "No" to all his suggestions –
but in the end she says "Yes".

Fill in the missing words and then read
the dialogue.

Peter Would you like to go to a restaurant
tonight?

Susan No, I don't think so.

Peter Well, would you ....

.... the theatre?

Susan No, I ....

Peter Well, ...

.... the cinema?

Susan No, ...

Peter Well, ...

....?

Susan Oh yes, good idea!

Peter Good. Let's go, then.

Four

I'd like to go to the cinema

Read this dialogue.

Penny Shall we go to the theatre tonight?
John Well, I'd like to go to the cinema.

Now look at the pictures and write the answers.

1 "Shall we go to the cinema tonight?"

"Well, I'd ....

...."

2 "Shall we go to a night club tonight?"

"..

...."

3 "Shall we go to a restaurant tonight?"

"..

...."

5 "Shall we go to the theatre tonight?"

"..

...."

4 "Shall we go to a pub tonight?"

"..

...."

6 ".. a concert ....?"

"..

...."

Five

Role play

You are going out with a friend tonight.
Look at "Tonight in London" and make plans.
Your friend will suggest things and you can make suggestions, too.
Your teacher will give you more information.

serious ['sɪərɪəs] ernst(haft)
entertainment [entə'teɪnmənt] Unterhaltung
friendly ['frendlɪ] freundlich, gemütlich
expensive [ɪk'spensɪv] teuer
reasonable ['riːznəbl] vernünftig, angemessen
trouble ['trʌbl] Schwierigkeit(en), Sorge(n), Verdruß
p.m. [piː'em] nachmittags
a.m. [eɪ'em] vormittags

UNIVERSAL SERVICES
Tonight in London

THEATRES

The New
"Two Friends" with Michael Moore and Ann Mitchell.
We think: An interesting and serious play about two old people.

The Palladium
"Words and Music" with Jean Atkins and Ronnie Oakes.
We think: A first-class musical. Good family entertainment.

CONCERTS

The Albert Hall
Mozart Concert
The London Symphony Orchestra
We think: First Class

The Band Wagon
Pete Armour and the Beatmen
Rock'n'roll.
We think: Noisy but good fun. Not expensive.

RESTAURANTS

Black's Grill
We think: Traditional English food and a friendly atmosphere. Expensive.

The Chung Ho
We think: A good restaurant for people who like *real* Chinese food. Not very expensive.

Antonio's
We think: Very good Italian food. Typical Italian atmosphere. Reasonable prices.

STRIP CLUBS

Lady Jane's
We think: The best strip club in town—but *very* expensive drinks.

NIGHT CLUBS

Downstairs 10 p.m. —4 a.m.
We think: Good small orchestra. Good floor show. Expensive.

Peter's Disco
We think: Young atmosphere. Good music. A good disco but expensive.

CINEMAS

Studio One
"Gone with the Wind" with Vivien Leigh, Clark Gable and Leslie Howard.
We think: If you haven't seen it, go and see it now. If you have seen it, go and see it again!

The Academy
"Two's Trouble". A comedy with Albert Robins and Gloria Ashley.
We think: Good family entertainment.

Six

Dialogues

Read these two short dialogues.

    Man What do you think of English television?
Woman It's very good.

    Man What do you think of Chinese food?
Woman It isn't very interesting.

Now ask and answer like this.
Here are some things to ask about and some words to answer with:

Ask about	*Answer with*
English beer	good
French food	bad
German television	interesting
Italian food	nice
your job	difficult
this book	easy
this exercise	expensive

Seven

Crossword

Do this crossword puzzle
– and find the hidden word.

1 Let's go to the . . . and see a comedy.
2 See you at the . . . for a drink.
3 There's a good film on at the . . .
4 The . . . opens at 10 o'clock.
5 He's a waiter at a . . .
6 Lady Jane's is a . . .
7 Shall we watch . . . tonight?
8 I'd like to go to the Bach . . .

Eight

Translate these sentences

Translate these sentences into German.
Use idiomatic German.

1 Where's the bank?
2 Would you like to go to the cinema?
3 I'd like to see a musical.
4 No, I don't think so.
5 Shall we go to the theatre tonight?

Now translate these sentences into English.
Try not to look at the sentences above.

6 Würdest du gern ins Theater gehen?
7 Ich würde gern eine Komödie sehen.
8 Wo ist das Postamt?
9 Nein, ich glaube nicht.
10 Wollen wir heute abend in den Pub gehen?

> **beer** [bɪə] Bier
> **difficult** ['dɪfɪkəlt] schwer, schwierig

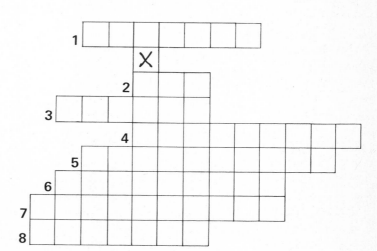

Marco – an Italian waiter

"My name's Marco. I work at Antonio's, an Italian restaurant in Soho. I'm from Naples, really, but there isn't any work in Naples, so I came to London.

I got a job as a waiter at Antonio's. My brother works here, too. But the pay isn't very good, and the hours are long. Still, it's a job. And it's not a bad restaurant. The food's good and it's got a good atmosphere. So most nights we're full. It isn't very expensive, really. But I guess that Mr Antonio makes a lot of money."

Right or wrong?

1 Marco had a job in Naples.
2 Marco's brother works at Antonio's.
3 The pay isn't bad.
4 Marco works long hours.
5 He likes the atmosphere in the restaurant.
6 The food is good but expensive.
7 The restaurant is popular.
8 Marco is a cook.

Naples ['neɪplz] Neapel
pay [peɪ] Bezahlung, Verdienst
the hours [ðɪ 'aʊəz] die Arbeitszeit
we're full [wɪə 'fʊl] wir sind voll (besetzt)

Opinions
What would you like to do tomorrow evening?

Peter Winter, 29, teacher
"I'd like to go to the cinema."

Anne Dixon, 28, typist
"I'd like to go out with some friends."

Jean Stone, 40, shop assistant
"I'd like to stay at home and watch television."

4. A phone call for

The telephone rings in John Austin's flat.
It is Wednesday afternoon.

John Hullo, John Austin.

Girl Hullo, John. It's me.

John Oh, hullo. Who's *me*?

Girl It's me, Monique. You know.

John Oh, yes, Monique! Hullo. Where are you?

Monique I'm in Paris, of course.
Listen. I'm coming to London on Saturday.

John Are you? Oh, wonderful. What time?

Monique Eleven twenty. It's Flight AF 782.

John Eleven twenty, Flight AF 782. Right.

John

John Shall we have lunch at the airport?
Monique Oh no! Let's go to that nice Italian restaurant. You know. What's its name?
John Oh, Antonio's. Good idea.
Monique Fine. See you on Saturday at the airport, then. Bye-bye.
John Bye!
Oh my God! Life *is* complicated!

phone call ['fəʊn kɔːl] Telefonanruf, -gespräch
of course [əv 'kɔːs] natürlich
flight [flaɪt] Flug
complicated ['kɒmplɪkeɪtɪd] kompliziert

"Life *is* complicated!"

How to say it

Asking for and giving information; making suggestions

1

I'm coming to (I am) leaving John's going to He's (He is) leaving Monique's coming to She's (She is) leaving	London Paris Bradford London London Paris	on Tuesday. at 9.30. on Thursday. at 11 o'clock. at 11.20 on Tuesday.	Are you? Is he? Is she?

● Gr 27 C, 29, 34 ● Ex 3,4

Make sentences like this. Work in pairs.

2

Where	are you?		I'm in ...
Where's	John? Monique? my passport? your ticket? Monique's ticket? her ticket? John's wallet? his wallet?		He's in ... She's in ... It's over there. It's here.

● Gr 36 ● Ex 2, 8

Now make questions like this. Work in pairs.

3

What's the time?	It's ten o'clock. It's ten thirty.

● Gr 36

Now ask the time. Work in pairs.

4

Let's	go to the cinema. go to the theatre. go to Antonio's. go home.	Good idea.

● Gr 11, 16

Make suggestions like this.

Phrases

Practise saying these phrases.

You know!
Of course.
Right.
See you on ...
Listen.

Wonderful!
Fine!
Bye-bye.
Bye.
(See Ex 1.)

Numbers

thirteen 13 – fourteen 14
fifteen 15 – sixteen 16
seventeen 17 – eighteen 18
nineteen 19 – twenty 20
thirty 30 – forty 40 – fifty 50.
● Gr 18

---

ticket ['tɪkɪt] (Flug-, Fahr-, Eintritts-)Karte
wallet ['wɒlɪt] Brieftasche

Exercises

One

Pairs

Put the sentences in A together with the right sentences in B

A 1 See you on Monday, then.
2 I'm coming to Stockholm on Saturday.
3 It's Flight **BA 339**.
4 Who's Penny?
5 Let's go to that nice Chinese restaurant.

B 1 Yes. Bye-bye.
2 Oh, wonderful!
3 She's John's girl friend.
4 **BA 339**. Right.
5 Good idea!

Two

Telephone conversation

Read this telephone conversation.

Ethel Hullo, it's Ethel.
Jack Hullo. Where are you?
Ethel I'm at the airport.

Now you ring a friend.
You can be at the station
the office
the hotel/the Royal Hotel
the theatre/the Lyric
the cinema/the Odeon
the bus station
the restaurant/Antonio's

Three

What time?

Read this conversation.

Monique I'm coming to London on Saturday.
John What time?
Monique Ten thirty.
John Good. See you at the airport.

Now you write, and then read, with a friend
what these people say:

Four

John Austin's diary

Say what John is doing this week.

For example: He's going to Bradford on Sunday.

SUNDAY	9.00 a.m.	*Bradford*
MONDAY	2.00 p.m.	*Birmingham*
TUESDAY	6.00 p.m.	*Stoke*
WEDNESDAY	8.00 a.m.	*Manchester*
THURSDAY	3.00 p.m.	*Leeds*
FRIDAY	4.00 p.m.	*York*
SATURDAY	10.00 a.m.	*London*

Now say what he is doing again, like this:
He's going to Bradford on Sunday morning at
9 o'clock.
He's going to Birmingham on Monday afternoon
at 2 o'clock.

---

diary ['daɪərɪ] Tagebuch, Kalender
a.m. [eɪ'em] vormittags
p.m. [pi:'em] nachmittags

Five

Flight Numbers

Write out these Flight Numbers in words.
Then say them.

BA 159   *one five nine*

AF 873   ....

LH 782   ....

BA 246   ....

AF 541   ....

LH 673   ....

BA 898   ....

Six

Role play

You are in another country.
You phone a friend to tell him that you
are coming to see him.
Your teacher will give you more information.

Seven

Write the words

Write the missing words in the sentences.
Use the words in the box.

Flight going at is on in

"I'm .... to London .... Thursday.

I'll be .... London .... 10.15.

The .... Number .... LH 828."

Eight

Where's my passport?

Read these conversations.

He Where's my passport?
She It's over there.

She Where's my bag?
He It's here.

Now look at the words in the box.
Write the right words under the pictures.

> my bag   my watch   my wallet   my handbag
> the money   the brochure   the ticket

1 .... 2 .... 3 ....

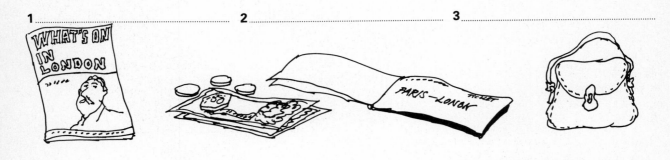

4 .... 5 .... 6 .... 7 ....

Now use the words to have conversations like those above.

Nine

Translate these sentences

Translate these sentences into German.
Use idiomatic German.

1 Where are you?
2 It's me.
3 I'm coming to Copenhagen on Monday morning.
4 See you at the airport.
5 Life is complicated!

Now translate these sentences into English.
Try not to look at the sentences above.

6 Ich komme am Dienstag nachmittag nach London.
7 Wir sehen uns im Restaurant.
8 Ich bin es.
9 Wo ist er?
10 Englisch ist kompliziert.

Ten

Who is going where?

Look at the bags, the names and the colours.
Read the text below, and then fill in the names and destinations.
For example: little black bag – Miss Dupont – Paris

Miss Dupont has a little black bag.
The man with the red bag is going to New York.
Mrs Potter's bag isn't brown. It's white.
Dr Schrand is going to Bonn.
Mr Dean has a red bag.
Miss Dupont is going to Paris.
The woman with the white bag is going to Lisbon.
The big black bag is Dr Schrand's.
Hans Borg is going to Oslo. What colour is his bag?

It's ....

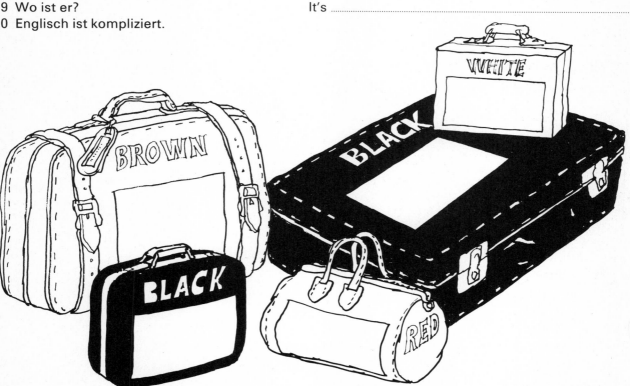

Read this

London to New[
in six seconds

George Rolls worked in New York for six months. Back in London, he got an enormous telephone bill for £250! But he wasn't surprised. Why not?

Because his wife had phoned him every morning to wake him up!

Nowadays it is so easy to ring all over the world. In fact, you can dial direct to almost every town in Europe.

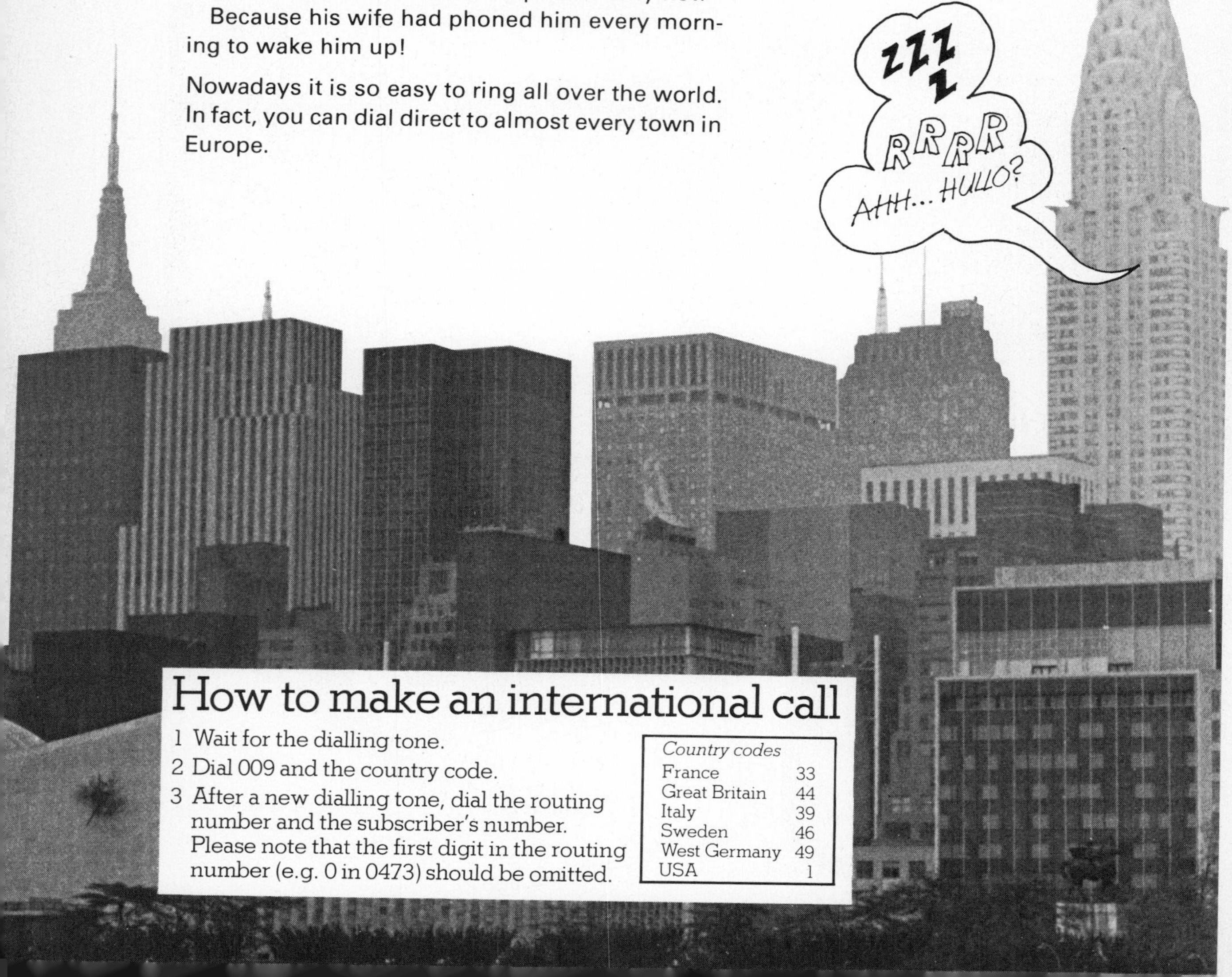

ZZZ Z

RRRR

AHH... HULLO?

How to make an international call

1 Wait for the dialling tone.
2 Dial 009 and the country code.
3 After a new dialling tone, dial the routing number and the subscriber's number. Please note that the first digit in the routing number (e.g. 0 in 0473) should be omitted.

Country codes	
France	33
Great Britain	44
Italy	39
Sweden	46
West Germany	49
USA	1

Opinions

What are you doing this weekend?

Carol White, 42, housewife
"I'm going to a party on
Saturday."

Martin Rose, 59, shopkeeper
"I'm going to my country
cottage."

Monica Horn, 25, factory worker
"Nothing special."

Right or wrong?

1 George Rolls lives in London.
2 He is not married.
3 His wife phoned him to say Good night.
4 George was not surprised about his phone bill.
5 When you phone to Great Britain,
   you dial 00946 first.
6 A person who has a telephone is a subscriber.
7 The first number you dial when you make an
   international call is the routing number.

> **bill** [bɪl] Rechnung
> **surprised** [səˈpraɪzd] überrascht
> **dial** [ˈdaɪəl] (eine Nummer) wählen
> **routing number** [ˈruːtɪŋ ˈnʌmbə] Ortsnetzkennzahl
> **subscriber** [səbˈskraɪbə] Teilnehmer
> **digit** [ˈdɪdʒɪt] Ziffer
> **omit** [əˈmɪt] aus-, weglassen
> **country cottage** [ˈkʌntrɪ ˈkɒtɪdʒ] Landhaus

Would you like to meet a new friend?

Come and talk to
UNIVERSAL SERVICES
We can help you!
Phone 01-908-3214
for a personal interview.

"Your problem is our problem."

At Universal Services' London office. It is Thursday morning.

John	Good morning. Are you Miss Harrison?
Miss H	Yes, that's right.
John	Please come in.
Miss H	Thank you.
John	Please sit down.
Miss H	Thank you.
John	Cigarette?
Miss H	No, thank you. I don't smoke.

rests?

John	Now, you would like to meet a new friend, Miss Harrison?
Miss H	Yes.
John	Can I ask you a few questions?
Miss H	Yes, of course.
John	First, what are your interests?
Miss H	Interests? Well, I like my work. I'm a chemical engineer.
John	An engineer. That's interesting. Mmmm. Do you like sport, Miss Harrison?
Miss H	Yes, I do. I like judo.
John	Judo, I see. What about books?
Miss H	No, I don't like reading much.
John	I see. Do you like the theatre?
Miss H	No, not much. But I like going to the cinema.
John	Good.
Miss H	Oh, and I like going out to dinner.
John	I see. Er, can I ask you to fill in this form, please?
Miss H	Oh, yes, certainly.

---

interest ['ɪntrɪst] Interesse
a few [ə'fjuː] ein paar
chemical engineer ['kemɪkl endʒɪ'nɪə] Chemotechniker (in)
fill in a form [fɪl 'ɪn ə 'fɔːm] ein Formular ausfüllen

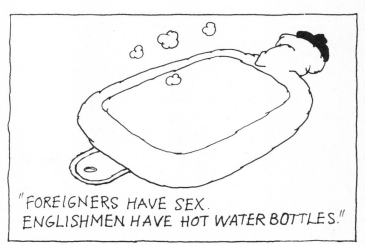

"FOREIGNERS HAVE SEX.
ENGLISHMEN HAVE HOT WATER BOTTLES."

George Mikes: How to be an alien.

How to say it

Asking about interests; likes and dislikes; asking polite questions

1

Do you like	sport? books? music? reading? going to the cinema? going to the theatre?

Yes, I do. No, I don't. (do not) No, not very much.

Now make questions. Work in pairs.

• Gr 24, 25 A, 27 B, 29, 31
• Ex 2

2

I like	my work. judo. jazz. dancing. cooking. going to the theatre.

Do you? So do I. Do you? I don't.

Now make sentences like this. Work in pairs.

• Gr 27 C, 28, 29, 31 • Ex 2, 4, 5

3

I don't like	football cooking Chinese food swimming	very much.

Don't you? Don't you? I do. Nor do I.

Now make sentences like this. Work in pairs.

• Gr 26, 27 C, 31
• Ex 2,3

4

Can I	ask you a few questions? ask you to fill in this form? speak to Mr Austin?

Yes, of course.

Now ask questions like this. Work in pairs.

• Gr 25 B

Phrases

Practise saying these phrases

Good morning.
Good afternoon.
Good evening.
Good night.
Goodbye.
Mmmm.
Well, . . .
I see.
Yes, of course.
Oh.
Er . . .
(See Ex 1.)

Numbers

sixty 60 — seventy 70 —
eighty 80 — ninety 90 —
a hundred 100
a thousand 1,000 —
a million 1,000,000.

• Gr 18

cooking ['kʊkɪŋ] Kochen
nor do I [nɔːdʊ 'aɪ] ich auch nicht

Exercises

One

Pairs

Put the sentences in A together with the right sentences in B.

A 1 Good afternoon.
2 Do you like jazz?
3 I'd like to meet a new friend.
4 Please sit down.
5 Goodbye.

B 1 No, not very much.
2 I see.
3 Good afternoon.
4 Thank you.
5 Goodbye.

Two

Interests

Look at the form below, "INTERESTS".
Please fill it in.
Write *I like* or *I don't like.*

Interests

Please write "I like" or "I don't like".

Sport

_____ football
_____ tennis
_____ skiing

_____ swimming
_____ watching football
· · · · · · · · · · · · · · ·
(other sport)

Entertainment

_____ going to the cinema
_____ going to the theatre
_____ pop music

_____ watching television
_____ dancing
· · · · · · · · · · · · · · ·
(other entertainment)

Food

_____ Italian food
_____ Chinese food
_____ French food

_____ English food
_____ eating at home
_____ cooking

Other interests

Please write down your interests:

I like _____   I don't like _____

_____   _____

Three

Suggestions

Say "No" to all these suggestions.

Example:
"Would you like to go to a Chinese restaurant? (Chinese food)
"No, I don't think so. I don't like Chinese food very much."

1 Would you like to go to a Spanish restaurant? (Spanish food)
2 Would you like to go to a Bach concert? (classical music)
3 Would you like to go to the Frank Zappa concert? (rock music)
4 Would you like to see "South Pacific"? (musicals)
5 Would you like to see "Chinatown"? (thrillers)
6 Would you like to go to a football match? (sport)
7 Would you like to watch the Song Contest? (pop music)
8 Would you like to go to a dinner dance? (dancing)

Four

Sports and games

Look at the pictures below.
Write the right words from the box
under each picture.

| play badminton play golf |
| play cards play chess |
| go riding go fishing |
| go swimming go skating |

Now read this dialogue between
a man and a girl at a party.
He is asking her about her interests.

"What do you do in your spare time?"
"I go riding."
"Do you? So do I!"

Now have a conversation like this
with a friend.
Look at the pictures, ask and answer.

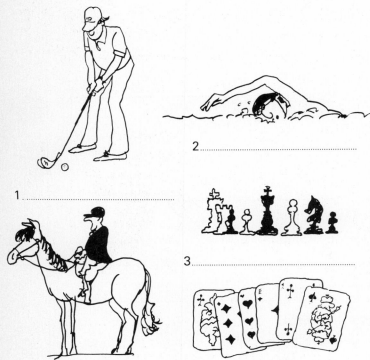

1 ....

2 ....

3 ....

5 ....

6 ....

7 ....

4 ....

8 ....

Five

Interests

Look at the pictures below.
Write the right words from the box under the pictures.

visiting museums	going for walks
visiting churches	dancing
visiting art galleries	listening to music

Two people are talking about what they like doing in their spare time.

"What do you do in your spare time?"
"I like going for walks."
"Do you? So do I."

Now have conversations with your partner like this. Look at the pictures, ask and answer.

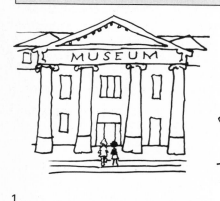 

1 .... 2 .... 3 ....

4 .... 5 .... 6 ....

---

chess [tʃes] Schach
go skating [gəʊ ˈskeɪtɪŋ] Schlittschuh laufen
spare time [ˈspeə taɪm] Freizeit

visit [ˈvɪzɪt] besuchen, besichtigen
go for walks [gəʊ fə ˈwɔːks] spazierengehen
art gallery [ˈɑːt gælərɪ] Kunstgalerie, -ausstellung

Six

Roleplay

You'd like a weekend holiday.
Go to Universal Services and ask for help.
Your teacher will give you more information.

Have a holiday this weekend.
We have four alternatives.

Phone or visit
UNIVERSAL SERVICES
7 Baker Street, London. Tel. 01-908-3214

UNIVERSAL SERVICES
Weekend holidays interview form

Do you like . . . . ?

A Culture
1 visiting churches
2 visiting museums
3 visiting art galleries
4 going to the theatre
5 going to concerts

C Food
1 French
2 Chinese
3 Italian
4 English

D Sports
1 going for walks
2 going fishing
3 going swimming
4 going sailing
5 going riding
6 playing tennis
7 playing golf

B Entertainment
1 going shopping
2 going sightseeing
3 dancing
4 going to night clubs

Seven

Translate these sentences

Translate these sentences into German.
Use idiomatic German.

1 Please come in.
2 I like swimming. – So do I.
3 I would like to meet Miss Boman.
4 Can I ask you to fill in this form?
5 What are your interests?

Now translate these sentences into English.
Try not to look at the sentences above.

6 Was haben Sie für Interessen?
7 Ich würde gern Herrn Baker treffen.
8 Ich tanze gern. — Ich auch.
9 Kommen Sie bitte herein.
10 Darf ich Sie bitten, Ihren Namen und Ihre
   Adresse einzutragen?

Eight

Crossword

Across

5 Wednesday, . . ., Friday.
7

9

11 Not a woman.
12 What time does the plane
    . . . to London?
13 See you . . . Monday.

Down

1 See you . . . the pub, then.
2 Can I ask you a . . .?
3 Who . . . that?
4 Where's . . . passport?
6

7 Planes can . . .
8 Let's go to an . . . gallery.
9

10 What time does the train . . .
    to Stockholm?

What is an Englishman?

What do foreigners think about the typical Englishman?

They think that all Englishmen drink tea. Of course, tea is popular in England. Strong tea, with milk and lots of sugar. But many English people prefer coffee nowadays.

They also think that all Englishmen drink beer and spend all their spare time in pubs. But in fact a lot of English people never drink beer, and never go into a pub.

A lot of Englishmen like watching football on Saturday afternoon. But a lot don't. They prefer fishing, for example.

What do the statistics say about the typical English family?

They live in a small house with a small garden in a large town in the south-east of England. They have two children. The husband is thirty-two. He works in an office. He works forty hours a week – when he is not on strike! The wife looks after the house and works part time in a shop. They have three weeks' holiday a year.

Opinions

What do you like doing at the weekend?

Jane Cross, 46, traffic warden
"I like going for a drive
in the car."

Pat Lane, 24, post office clerk
"I like going for long walks
in the country."

Alan Clark, 38, bus conductor
"I like getting up late
at the weekend.
When I'm not working."

Right or wrong?

1 English people drink tea without milk.
2 A lot of English people prefer coffee.
3 All Englismen drink beer.
4 They spend all their spare time in pubs.
5 Fishing is not a popular sport.
6 The typical Englishman lives in a small town.
7 He lives in the north of England.
8 He works a forty-hour week.

foreigner [ˈfɒrɪnə] Ausländer(in)
think about [ˈθɪŋk əbaʊt] denken über, halten von
strong [strɒŋ] stark
sugar [ˈʃʊɡə] Zucker
prefer [prɪˈfɜː] bevorzugen
spend [spend] ver-, zubringen
strike [straɪk] Streik
part time [ˈpɑːt taɪm] halbtags

6. Looking after a vis

Sheila Black, a well-known Australian writer, is coming to London this week. Universal Services are organising her visit and Mary Hudson is looking after her at the weekend. Mary bumps into John in a pub at lunch time on Monday.

Mary Oh, hullo, John. Can I ask you something?
John Of course. Would you like a drink?
Mary No thanks, I've got one.
John Well, what can I do for you?
Mary Well, Sheila Black is coming to London on Wednesday.
John Sheila Black? Who's she?
Mary You know – the Australian writer.
John Oh yes, I know!

...tor

John What's the problem?

Mary Well, I'm looking after her at the weekend. Can you suggest something nice we can do?

John Mmmm. How old is she?

Mary I'm not sure. About 45, I think.

John Oh. Does she like music?

Mary I think so. She plays the piano, you know.

John Does she? Well, you can take her to that Mozart concert on Saturday at the Albert Hall.

Mary Um, yes. Good idea. But what about Sunday? Er, I expect she likes parties.

John Well, let's have a party on Sunday, then.

Mary Thanks, John. You're an angel.

John Yes, I know. Cheers!

Mary Cheers!

---

visitor ['vɪzɪtə] Besucher(in), Gast
writer ['raɪtə] Schriftsteller(in)
look after [lʊk 'ɑːftə] sich kümmern um
bump into [bʌmp 'ɪntə] (zufällig) treffen
suggest [sə'dʒest] vorschlagen
expect [ɪk'spekt] vermuten, annehmen

YOU'RE AN ANGEL!

How to say it

Asking about and talking about people

1

Does John like his work?	Yes, he does.
Does Mary like her work?	Yes, she does.
Does Pat like pop music?	
Does this bus stop at Waterloo?	Yes, it does.

● *Gr 24, 25, 26, 27 B* ● *Ex 2, 4, 6, 8*

Now ask questions like this.

2

Does Mrs Black like jazz?	No, she doesn't (does not).
Does Mary live in Sweden?	No, she doesn't.
Does John work at a restaurant?	No, he doesn't.
Does this bus stop at Euston?	No, it doesn't.

● *Gr 24, 25, 26, 27 B* ● *Ex 2, 4, 6, 8*

Now ask questions like this.
Then ask questions to get Yes and No answers.

3

| I like pop music. |
| I work at Universal Services. |
| I live in Germany. |
| I play the guitar. |

Mary like**s** pop music,	too.
John work**s** at Universal Services,	
Monica live**s** in Germany,	
Alan play**s** the guitar,	

● *Gr 28* ● *Ex. 2, 6, 7*

Note the **s** when Mary, Alan etc (**he**, **she**) are the subject.

Now say what you like and what you do, and talk about a third person.

4

| I don't (do not) like pop music. |
| I don't live in London. |
| I don't play the piano. |
| I don't know Peter. |

Mr Black doesn't like pop,	either.
Penny doesn't live in London,	
Peter doesn't play the piano,	
Monica doesn't know Peter,	

● *Gr 10, 26* ● *Ex 4, 6*

Now say what you don't like and what you don't do, and talk about a third person.

5

How old	is he?	About 35.
	is Peter?	About 50, I think.
	is she?	I'm not sure.
	is Mary?	I don't know.

Now ask questions like this. ● *Gr 36* ● *Ex 3*

Phrases

Practise saying these phrases.

Of course.   You know!   Oh yes, I know!
What's the problem?   I'm not sure.
I think so.   …, I think.   Cheers!
(See Ex 1.)

Numbers

a hundred 100 – a hundred and twenty-seven 127 –
three hundred 300 – five thousand 5,000 –
a hundred and eighty-five million 185,000,000 –
two thousand, six hundred and ninety-nine 2,699.

Exercises

One

Pairs

Put the sentences in A together with the right sentences in B.

A 1 Eric Spencer is coming tomorrow.
   2 Let's go to lunch.
   3 How old is Mrs Bruce?
   4 Does Peter play tennis?
   5 Can I come in?

B 1 Good idea.
   2 I think so.
   3 About ninety-nine, I think.
   4 Of course.
   5 Yes, I know.

Two

Ask and answer

Ask and answer questions like this:

A My father speaks French.

B *Does he speak German* , too? (German)

A *Yes, he does. (I'm not sure.) I don't think so.*

1 Ann plays the guitar.

.... too? (piano)

2 David likes French food.

.... , too? (Chinese)

3 Mrs Cross plays golf.

.... , too? (badminton)

4 My wife knows Mrs Cross.

.... , too? (Mr Cross)

5 Marco works on Saturdays.

.... , too? (Sundays)

6 The 10.20 train goes to Manchester.

.... , too? (Birmingham)

7 Flight **LH 064** goes to London.

.... , too? (Copenhagen)

8 This bus stops at Piccadilly Circus.

.... , too? (Trafalgar Square)

Three

How old?

Look at Alan Jackson. — How old is he, do you think?
Oh, about 45. 50, perhaps.

Now look at the other people and say how old you think they are.

Alan Jackson

Glenda Brian

Martha Roberts

Albert Hobbs

Joan Baker

Peter Brown

John Kidd

Mark Stevens

Four

My friend

Do you know your friends?
Think of a friend and try to answer these questions.
Another person in the group will ask you the questions.

Example:

Questions
Is your friend a man
or a woman?
Does he/she like music?

Answers
A man./A woman.
Yes, he/she does.
No, he doesn't.
I think so.
I don't think so.
I'm not sure.
I don't know.

Here are the questions:

How old is he/she?
Is he/she married/single/divorced?
Does he/she speak English well?
Does he/she like classical music?
Does he/she like Italian food?
Does he/she like travelling?
Does he/she like going to the theatre?
Does he/she like reading?
Does he/she play tennis?
Does he/she play the guitar?
Does he/she work in **Cologne**?
Who is it?

> **single** ['sɪŋgl] alleinstehend, unverheiratet
> **divorced** [dɪ'vɔːst] geschieden
> **travelling** ['trævlɪŋ] Reisen

Five

> # Role play
>
> You and a friend are planning some activities for a visitor.
> Talk about the visitor's interests and make suggestions.
> Your teacher will give you more information.

Six

The Hudsons

Read about Mary and Chris Hudson.

You know Mary Hudson. She works at Universal Services in London. She lives in Wembley with her husband Chris. Chris works at a bank near Marble Arch in the West End, but he goes to work by car. Mary goes to work by Underground. On Saturday afternoons Chris plays football, but Mary doesn't go and watch him. She thinks that football is a silly game. She goes swimming instead.

> **Wembley** ['wemblɪ] Stadtteil Londons
> **Marble Arch** ['mɑːbl 'ɑːtʃ] „Marmorbogen" nordöstlich von Hyde Park
> **the Underground** [ðɪ 'ʌndəgraʊnd] Londoner U-Bahn
> **silly** ['sɪlɪ] albern, lächerlich

Fill in Do and Does.

1 .... Chris work in a bank?

Yes, he ....

2 .... the Hudsons live in Wembley?

Yes, they ....

3 .... Chris work in the City?

No, he .... n't.

4 .... Mary and Chris work on Saturdays?

No, they .... n't.

5 .... Mary go to work by Underground?

Yes, she ....

6 .... Chris go to work by Underground too?

No, he .... n't.

7 .... Chris and Mary go swimming on

Saturday afternoons?

Well, Mary ...., but Chris .... n't.

Seven

Put it right

For example:

Mary Hudson works at a bank.

No she doesn't. She works at Universal Services.

1 Chris works at Universal Services.
2 He goes to work by Underground,
3 Mary goes to work by car.
4 On Saturday afternoons Chris goes swimming.
5 Mary goes to watch him play football.
6 Mary likes football.
7 Mary lives with her mother and father.
8 Chris lives in Birmingham.

Eight

Go by bus!

Mr Hudson goes to work by car – usually.
But today his car is at the garage.
And he does not know which bus to take to work.
So he asks Mary:

Does the 171 go to Marble Arch?
No, I don't think so.
Does the 15 go to Piccadilly Circus?
Yes, it does.

Now look at the bus information below and answer
questions like that.

Bus No.	Goes to
88	Marble Arch
24	Trafalgar Square
14	King's Cross
15	Piccadilly Circus
52	The Albert Hall
12	Oxford Circus
171	Waterloo

Nine

Translate these sentences

Translate these sentences into idiomatic German.

1 Can I come in?
2 John Black is coming to Nuremberg next week.
3 Does he like football?
4 I expect he likes pop music.
5 I don't know, I'm not sure.

Now translate these sentences into English.
Try not to look at the sentences above.

6 Alan kommt nächsten Dienstag nach Bonn.
7 Dürfen wir hereinkommen?
8 Ich nehme an, er mag chinesisches Essen.
9 Ich weiß es nicht, ich bin mir nicht sicher.
10 Liebt er klassische Musik?

Ten

Go by Underground!

How do you get to Embankment from Euston?
You take the Northern Line.

How do you get from Euston to Holborn?
You take the Northern Line to Tottenham Court Road and change to
the Central Line.

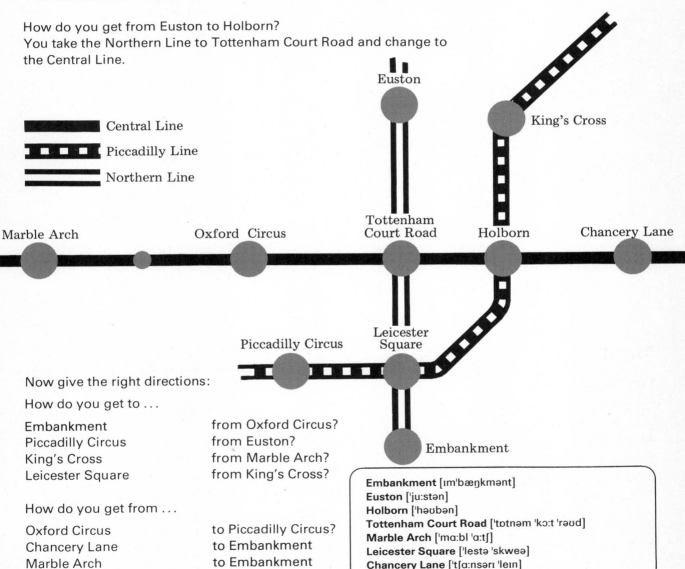

Central Line
Piccadilly Line
Northern Line

Euston

King's Cross

Marble Arch Oxford Circus

Tottenham
Court Road Holborn Chancery Lane

Piccadilly Circus

Leicester
Square

Embankment

Now give the right directions:

How do you get to . . .

Embankment	from Oxford Circus?
Piccadilly Circus	from Euston?
King's Cross	from Marble Arch?
Leicester Square	from King's Cross?

How do you get from . . .

Oxford Circus	to Piccadilly Circus?
Chancery Lane	to Embankment
Marble Arch	to Embankment
Piccadilly Circus	to Chancery Lane?

Embankment [ɪm'bæŋkmənt]
Euston ['ju:stən]
Holborn ['həʊbən]
Tottenham Court Road ['tɒtnəm 'kɔ:t 'rəʊd]
Marble Arch ['mɑ:bl 'ɑ:tʃ]
Leicester Square ['lestə 'skweə]
Chancery Lane ['tʃɑ:nsərɪ 'leɪn]

Australia

Right or wrong?

Try to say if these sentences are right or wrong. If you don't know, read the text about Australia and try again.

1. Australia is more than 25,000 kilometres from Europe.
2. It takes a day and a night to get there by plane.
3. It takes six weeks to get to Sydney by boat.
4. The United States is bigger than Australia.
5. Australia is much bigger than Europe.
6. The population is about 20 million.
7. Kangaroos and koala bears live there.
8. Australia is a republic.
9. The capital is Canberra.
10. Australia is developing rather slowly.

Australia is about 20,000 kilometres from Europe – it is right over the other side of the world. It takes about 24 hours to get to Sydney by air, and about a month to get there by sea.

Australia is a very large country. It is nearly as big as the United States or Europe. But the population is only about 12 million – compared with 400 million in Europe! And there are about 185 million in the United States.

What do Europeans know about Australia? Not very much! They probably know that it is winter there when it is summer here, and vice versa. And that those strange animals the kangaroos and the koala bears live there. But they probably think that Australia is a republic – and they are wrong. It recognises Queen Elizabeth as the Head of State. And they probably think that Sydney is the capital. Wrong again. It is Canberra. What they probably don't know is that Australia is developing very fast and will be a very powerful country by the year 2,000.

---

capital [ˈkæpɪtl] Hauptstadt
develop [dɪˈveləp] entwickeln
compared with [kəmˈpeəd wɪð] verglichen mit
strange [streɪndʒ] seltsam, fremd(artig)
recognise [ˈrekəgnaɪz] anerkennen
powerful [ˈpaʊəfʊl] mächtig, stark
accordion [əˈkɔːdjən] Ziehharmonika, Akkordeon

Opinions

What sort of music do you like best?

Duncan Bates, 21, student
"I like classical music best."

Pete Baxter, 68, pensioner
"I like accordion music."

Barbara Carter, 49, doctor
"I like all kinds of music."

7. A trip to Oxford

**Monique is in London now. She and John are at his flat.
She is going to see some friends at the weekend.**

John What about this family you're going
to see at the weekend?

Monique The Johnsons, you mean.
They live in Oxford now.
What's the best way to get there?

John Well, you can go by bus or by train.

Monique Oh, I think I'll go by train.
I don't like buses very much.

John Or you can hire a car, of course.

Monique How much is that?

John	Well, it depends. About £10 a day.
Monique	Oh, that's a lot. How much is the train?
John	Let's see. It's £4.40 return.
Monique	Oh, that's not too bad.
	I think I'll go by train.
	Can you get me the ticket?
John	Well, I can.
	But you can get it at the station, you know.
Monique	Okay.
John	Are you coming back on Saturday?
Monique	No, on Sunday evening.
John	Thank goodness. I mean, er ...
	Shall we have something to eat
	here on Sunday evening?
Monique	Yes, good idea. Thank you.

flat [flæt] Wohnung
the best way [ðə 'best 'weɪ] am besten
it depends [ɪt dɪ'pends] es kommt darauf an
return [rɪ'tɜːn] (hin und) zurück
Thank goodness! ['θæŋk 'gʊdnɪs] Gott sei
  Dank!

How to say it

Planning and deciding

1	I'm He's She's We're They're	going to	see a friend hire a car have a party play tennis meet at the pub	at the weekend. tomorrow. on Saturday. on Sunday. tonight.	Are you? Is he? Is she? Are we? Are they?

● Gr 33, 27 C ● Ex 3

Talk about your plans like this.

2	I think I'll	go by train. go by bus. hire a car. go to London.	All right. Okay.

● Gr 32 ● Ex 2, 3

Now say what you have decided.

3	You can	go by bus or by train. go by train or by car. go by plane or by boat. go by plane or by train. go by car or by bus.	I think I'll go by . . .

● Gr 32 ● Ex 2, 3, 4

Now say what the alternatives are, like this.

4	How much is it	to hire a car? to go by train? to send a letter to Germany? to send a postcard abroad?	About £10 a day. £4.40 return. Ten pence. Eight pence.

● Gr 36, 4 ● Ex 5

Now ask questions like this.

Phrases

Practise saying these phrases.

What about . . .?
It depends.
That's a lot.
That's not too bad.
Let's see.
Okay.
Thank goodness.
(See Ex 1.)

> **decide** [dɪ'saɪd] sich entscheiden, beschließen
> **abroad** [ə'brɔːd] ins Ausland

Exercises

One

Pairs

Put the sentences in A with the right sentences in B.

A 1 What's the name of that boy
      you play tennis with?
   2 What's on television tonight?
   3 It's going to be nice and warm tomorrow.
   4 Are you coming to the picnic?
   5 It's £20 to hire a Jaguar.

B 1 That's a lot.
   2 Thank goodness.
   3 Let's see.
   4 Well, it depends.
   5 Albert, you mean.

Two

The best way

You are in Hamburg.
Ask a friend the best way to get to these places.

Ask like this:

What's the best way to get to London?

to Rothenburg / Berlin / Tokyo / Oslo / the library /
Copenhagen / the town centre / Helsinki / New York

Answer like this:

By plane	By bus
By boat	By Underground
By train	By taxi
By car	

Example: What's the best way to get to New York?
          By plane.

Three

By train or by bus?

Read this dialogue:

Girl I'm going to see a friend in Birmingham on
      Saturday. What's the best way to get there?
Man Well, you can go by train or by bus.
Girl Oh, I think I'll go by bus.
      I don't like trains very much.

Now make more conversations like this.
Use the words in the boxes below.

Rothenburg	Saturday	by train	by car
Hanover	Sunday	by bus	by train
Paris	Monday	by train	by plane
Helsinki	Friday	by boat	by plane
New York	Thursday	by plane	by boat

Four

Transport

Put these words in pairs,
for example: train – railway station

bus	airport
plane	garage
taxi	air terminal
coach	Underground station
boat	bus stop
train	taxi rank
Underground	railway station
car	harbour

> **library** ['laɪbrərɪ] Bücherei, Bibliothek

Five

Car Hire   Study this brochure.

UNIVERSAL SERVICES
CAR HIRE

We have the latest models of
VOLVO, AUDI, FORD ESCORT

We also have luxury and sports cars.
The following rates include

Hire, full insurance, 500 miles free mileage

Cars must be returned by midnight on the last
day of hire.

	1 day	2 days	3 days	1 week
VOLVO 244	£11	£20	£30	£50
AUDI 100	£9	£16	£24	£45
ESCORT	£7	£12	£18	£35

Luxury and sports cars (Rolls Royce, Jaguar):
Please ask for the special rates.

Now ask and answer questions like this:
How much is it to hire an AUDI for three days?
It's £24.

Six

Dialogue

Read and practise this dialogue.

Woman   Good morning. I'd like to hire a car.
Man   Yes, madam. When do you want it?
Woman   Tomorrow.
Man   How many days?
Woman   Three.
Man   I see. Er . . . you can have an Escort or
a Volvo.
Woman   I see. I think I'll have an Escort, please.
How much is it?
Man   An Escort for three days. That's £18.
Woman   That's fine. Thank you.

Seven

Role play

You are going to see some friends and
you want to hire a car.
Go to the UNIVERSAL SERVICES CAR HIRE
Office and hire a car.
Your teacher will give you more
information.

Eight

A postcard

Look at the words above the postcard
and fill in the gaps.

but	isn't very good	week
going to	the	are
here	today	
I'm	town	

Dear Jim,
As you can see .... here in Oxford
.... I'm visiting .... Johnsons.
They .... the family I was an au pair
girl with. This afternoon we're ....
.... have a picnic. The weather ....
.... , I'm afraid, ... Oxford
is a beautiful ....
Wish you were .... See you next ....
Love,
Monique

Jim
c/o
6 rue
75 F
F

rate [reɪt] Gebühr, Preis
insurance [ɪnˈʃʊərəns] Versicherung
500 miles free mileage [ˈfaɪv ˈhʌndrəd ˈmaɪlz friː ˈmaɪlɪdʒ] die ersten 800 km sind frei
gap [gæp] Lücke
wish [wɪʃ] wünschen
order [ˈɔːdə] Reihenfolge

Nine

Translate these sentences

Translate these sentences into German.
Use idiomatic German.

1 The Johnsons live in Oxford.
2 You can go by bus or by car.
3 How much is it?
4 Are you coming back on Monday morning?
5 Well, it depends.

Now translate these sentences into English.
Try not to look at the German sentences above.

6 Kommst du am Freitag abend zurück?
7 Man kann mit dem Auto oder Bus fahren.
8 Was kostet es?
9 Nun, das kommt darauf an.
10 Die Wilsons wohnen in Manchester.

Ten

A conversation

Put the words in the boxes in the right order
and make a conversation.

For example:
Man I'm going to Birmingham on Friday.

Man	*Woman*	*Man*	*Woman*	*Man*	*Woman*	*Man*
Friday.	train?	No,	it	think.	lot!	know,
to	going	a	much	About	a	I
I'm	Are	think	How	pounds	That's	Yes,
Birmingham	by	car.	hire	I		but
on	you	hire	to	ten		trains.
going		I	is			like
		I'll	car?			I
			a			don't

A letter

Monique was an au pair girl in England two years ago.
This is a letter from Mrs Johnson, two years ago, to her friend June.

15, Cross Street
Tring
10th Oct

Dear June,

I must tell you about our new au pair. She's a nice young French girl, Monique. She's very good. She cleans the house and does the shopping and looks after the children. But I do the cooking. She goes to English lessons two evenings a week, on Tuesdays and Thursdays. But there's just one thing. It's the telephone. She phones her boy friend in Paris every weekend, and she talks for hours!! Perhaps she's homesick. She never pays for the calls. Our telephone bill is going to be enormous!! I must teach her the phrase "Reverse the charges".

Well, I must stop now.
Best wishes,
Sandra

Mrs June Baxter,
3, South Terrace,
Littlehampton.
BN17 5NZ
Sussex.

Right or wrong?

1 Mrs Johnson thinks that Monique is a good au pair.
2 Monique does the cooking.
3 Mrs Johnson does the shopping.
4 Monique goes to English classes on Tuesday afternoons.
5 She phones her mother in Paris every weekend.
6 She pays for most of the calls.
7 Mrs Johnson wants her to pay for all the calls.

---

clean the house [ˈkliːn ðə ˈhaʊs] saubermachen
do the cooking [ˈduː ðə ˈkʊkɪŋ] kochen
for hours [fər ˈaʊəz] stundenlang
be homesick [bɪ ˈhəʊmsɪk] an Heimweh leiden
reverse the charges [rɪˈvɜːs ðə ˈtʃɑːdʒɪz] Gebühren zahlt der Angerufene

---

Opinions

How do you go to work?

Alison Burke, 60, district nurse
"I go to work by car."

Tom Driver, 44, fisherman
"I go to work by bus."

Elsie James, 53, librarian
"I walk to work."

Mary Hudson arranges sightseeing tours at the London office.

Mary   Good morning. Can I help you?

Man   Yes, I'd like to go on a tour.

Mary   I see. Where would you like to go?

Man   To the South Coast.

Mary   I see. Well, we've got a tour to Hastings and Brighton today, and a tour to the Isle of Wight on Wednesday.

Man   The Isle of Wight, I think. How much is it?

Mary   £6.

Man   What time is it?

Mary   Ten o'clock.

Man   Good. Can you book two tickets for me, please.

Mary   Certainly.

UNIVERSAL SERVICES

sightseeing

We arrange the following tours

**Round London
To Scotland
To the West Country
To the South Coast
To Shakespeare Country**

Please ask for further details of times, days and prices.

Universal Services,
7 Baker Street, London.
Tel 01-908-3214.

"Your problem is our problem."

like to go?

Mary Good afternoon. Can I help you?
Woman Yes, I'd like to go on a tour.
Mary I see. Where would you like to go?
Woman Well, to Stratford, perhaps.
Mary I see. We've got a tour to Stratford tomorrow.
Woman No, that's no good, I'm afraid.
What about Sunday?
Mary Yes, we've got a tour to Stratford and Oxford on Sunday.
Woman Good. How much is it?
Mary £6.
Woman And what time is it?
Mary Seven o'clock in the morning.
Woman I see. Can you book three tickets for me, please?
Mary Certainly.

---

further details [ˈfɜːðə ˈdiːteɪlz] weitere Einzelheiten
certainly [ˈsɜːtnlɪ] sicher, gewiß
perhaps [pəˈhæps] vielleicht

How to say it

Arranging days, times and places; asking for help

1

I'd (I would) We'd	like to	go on a tour. go to Oxford. go to Scotland.

When would you like	to go? to stop for coffee? to have lunch?

Ask questions like this. Work in pairs.

● Gr 35, 37 ● Ex 2

2

I'm going on holiday. Ann's going to France. John's going to America. We're going abroad. The Wilsons are going on a business trip.

Where to? When?	Paris. New York. Russia. Tomorrow. Next week.

Make conversations like this. Work in pairs.

● Gr 34, 36, 37

3

Can you	help me, tell me the time, give me a light, book two tickets,	please?	Certainly. Of course.

Ask questions like this. Work in pairs.

● Gr 25 B

4

What time does	the Oxford tour leave? it get there? John start work? the film start?	At 11 o'clock. At 12.30. At a quarter to nine. At a quarter past six.

Ask questions like this. Work in pairs.

● Gr 36 ● Ex 5

5

We've got (We have got)	a tour to Oxford a holiday a meeting a party	on Tuesday morning. on Wednesday afternoon. on Thursday evening. on Saturday at 8 o'clock.	Good. That's no good, I'm afraid.

Now make conversations like this. Work in pairs.

● Gr 23 ● Ex 3, 4

Phrases

Practise saying these phrases.

Can I help you?
Perhaps. Good.

That's no good, I'm afraid.
Certainly.
Today. Tomorrow.

(See Ex 1.)

> **go abroad** [gəʊ əˈbrɔːd] ins Ausland fahren
> **business trip** [ˈbɪznɪs trɪp] Geschäftsreise

Exercises

One

Pairs

Put the sentences in A with the right sentences in B.

A 1 Can you give me a light, please?
2 Do you think it's going to rain?
3 The taxi's here.
4 Can I help you?
5 There's a plane at 7 o'clock on Sunday morning.

B 1 That's no good, I'm afraid.
2 Certainly.
3 Good.
4 Yes, I'd like two tickets for tonight's concert.
5 Perhaps.

Two

I'd like to go to Scotland

Look at the map on page 76.
Say where you would like to go, like this:

A I'd like to go to Scotland.
B Would you? I'd like to go to Stratford.
A All right, then. Let's go to Stratford.

Three

John's diary

Here is a page of John Austin's diary.

Monday	Sightseeing tour to Oxford - 10
Tuesday	Committee meeting - 11.30
Wednesday	Sales conference - 9.15
Thursday	Party at Sally's - 7.30
Friday	Meeting with Mr Briggs - 9.45
Saturday	Football match - 2. Party for Jane - 8
Sunday	Concert - 5.30

Ask and answer questions like this:

A When is the sightseeing tour to Oxford?
B It's on Monday at 10.

diary ['daɪərɪ] Tagebuch, Kalender

Four

Your diary

Write your diary for next week, like John's.

Monday

Tuesday

Wednesday

Thursday

Friday

Saturday

Sunday

Five

Train time-table

Look at this train time-table for trains from London to the North of England.

KING'S CROSS	DONCASTER	LEEDS	HARROGATE	BRADFORD
01.15	04.30	05.12	07.38 **a**	06.47 **a**
10.15	13.03	13.45	–	14.30 **a**
14.20	17.17	18.00	18.48 **a**	18.30 **a**
18.04	20.20	21.00	21.45 **a**	21.37
22.50	01.58	02.45	–	03.33
a Change at Leeds				

time-table ['taɪmteɪbl] Fahrplan
passenger ['pæsɪndʒə] Reisende(r)
Doncaster ['dɒŋkəstə]
Harrogate ['hærəgɪt]

Passenger What time does the 01.15 from King's Cross get to Doncaster?
Clerk At 04.30.
Passenger Thank you.

Passenger What time does the 20.20 from Doncaster get to Harrogate?
Clerk At 21.45. Change at Leeds.
Passenger Thank you.

Now you are the passenger. Ask about the times of other trains.

Six

Role play

You would like to go on a tour.
Go to Universal Services.
Your teacher will give you more information.

Seven

Translate these sentences

Translate these sentences into idiomatic German.

1 Where would you like to go?
2 We've got a tour to Brighton on Tuesday afternoon.
3 Today at 5 o'clock.
4 Yes, that's all right.
5 No, that's no good, I'm afraid.

Now translate these sentences into English.
Try not to look at the German sentences above.

6 Wohin möchten Sie fahren?
7 Ich fürchte, das wird nicht gehen.
8 Ja, das paßt gut.
9 Wir haben einen Ausflug nach Wales am Vormittag.
10 Am Mittwoch morgen um 10.

Eight

A map of Britain

Find the right names of the towns,
and put them on the map of Britain.

1 NDLNOO   5 FROXDO
2 BUHRGNDEI   6 THAB
3 IGRHOBTN   7 GNISTASH
4 TARTSDORF   8 ESDEL

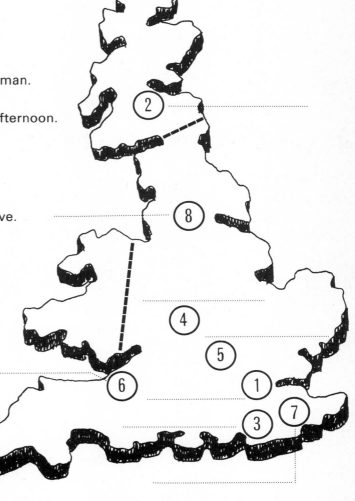

The Englishman the Welshman and

An Irishman dies, and his three friends, an Englishman, a Welshman and a Scotsman, come to his funeral.

Just before the coffin goes down, the Englishman – a perfect gentleman – says,

"Dear Patrick, I owe you £5."

And he takes a £5 note out of his wallet and puts it on the coffin.

The Welshman also wants to be a perfect gentleman, so he says,

"Patrick, I owe you £5, too."

And he takes a £5 note out of his wallet and puts it on the coffin.

The Scotsman says,

"That's right, my dear old friend, I owe you £5, too."

So he takes out his cheque book and his pen, writes out a cheque for £15, puts it on the coffin, picks up the two £5 notes and puts them in his wallet.

the Irishman, the Scotsman

Right or wrong?

1 The Welshman dies.
2 Four friends come to the funeral.
3 The Scotsman is a perfect gentleman.
4 The Englishman owes Patrick £5.
5 The Welsman puts five £1 notes on the coffin.
6 The Scotsman puts three £5 notes on the coffin.
7 The Englisman picks up £10 and puts it in his wallet.
8 The Scotsman writes a cheque to Patrick for £15.

> **funeral** [ˈfjuːnərəl] Begräbnis
> **coffin** [ˈkɒfɪn] Sarg
> **owe** [əʊ] schulden, schuldig sein
> **wallet** [ˈwɒlɪt] Brieftasche
> **car salesman** [ˈkɑː seɪlzmən] Autoverkäufer
> **art** [ɑːt] Kunst

Opinions

Where would you like to go for your summer holiday?

Bob Wood, 45, car salesman
"I'd like to tour Scotland by car."

Louise Short, 22, art student
"I'd like to hitch-hike round Europe."

Peter Potter, 60, plumber
"I'd like to fly round the world — first class."

9. A new flat

John is talking to Mrs Travers, an old friend of the family. They are standing in the street.

TO LET
FOLK & RD
HAYWARD

ALFRED MARKS
BUREAU

LET BY

84

Mrs Travers You've got a new flat, I hear.

John Yes, that's right.

Mrs Travers Where is it?

John In Baker Street – near the office.

Mrs Travers That's handy. What's it like?

John Well, it's not very big – just two rooms, a kitchen, and a bathroom. On the first floor.

Mrs Travers How nice! Is it in a new block of flats?

John No, it's quite old, actually. It's very nice, but it's a bit noisy.

Mrs Travers Still, it *is* near your office, isn't it?

John Yes, that's the best thing about it.

Mrs Travers And how's your girl friend? Sally, isn't it?

John Er, no, it's Penny, actually. She's fine, thanks.

THERE'S NO PLACE LIKE HOME

> **handy** ['hændɪ] praktisch, bequem
> **block of flats** ['blɒk əv 'flæts] Wohnblock
> **noisy** ['nɔɪzɪ] laut

How to say it

Describing homes

1

I've got (I have got) We've got They've got	a new flat. an old flat. a small flat. a big house.	Have you? Have they?
He's got (He has got) She's got	a new girl friend. a good job. a nice flat.	Has he? Has she?
It's got	four bedrooms.	Has it?

● Gr 23, 27 C ● Ex 2

Now make questions and answers like this.
Work in pairs.

2

Where's (Where is) Where is	your flat? his office? her hotel? it?	It's It's	in .... Street. in a new block of flats. in the centre of town. in .... Street.
Where are	the toilets? the glasses? they?	They're	downstairs. on the left. upstairs on the right.

Now make questions and answers like this. ● Gr 9, 36 ● Ex 6,7

3

Is	your flat it	in Baker Street? near your office? very expensive? in an old block of flats?	Yes. Yes, it is. No. No, it isn't.
Are	the rooms they	very big? comfortable? nice and sunny? very small?	Yes. Yes, they are. No. No, they aren't.

Now make questions and answers like this. ● Gr 22, 27 B

4

What's	your flat it	like?	It's	nice. modern. old-fashioned.
What are	the rooms they	like?	They're	not very big. nice and sunny.

● Gr 36 ● Ex 2,

Phrases
Practise saying these phrases.

... I hear.   How nice!
... actually   Still, ...
upstairs   downstairs
That's the best thing about it.
(See Ex 1.)

Prepositions
in the street
in Baker Street
in a new block of flats
in the centre of town
in the cupboard
in the bedroom
in the corner

on the first floor
on the left
on the right
on the floor
on the table

near the office
near the shopping centre

comfortable [ˈkʌmfətəbl] bequem
old-fashioned [əʊldˈfæʃənd] unmodern

Exercises

One

Pairs

Put the sentences in A with the right sentences in B.

A 1 I've got a new flat.
     2 Is it very old-fashioned?
     3 Where's the toilet?
     4 You've got a new car, I hear.
     5 They've got a very small house.

B 1 Upstairs in the bathroom, on the right.
     2 How nice!
     3 Yes, it's a Morris.
     4 Still, it's near the shopping centre.
     5 No, actually it's quite modern.

Two

What's it like?

Tell a friend about your flat or house, like this:

John I've got a two-room flat.
Sally Have you? What's it like?
John It's very nice.

Helen We've got a house with three
         bedrooms.
Karen Have you? What's it like?
Helen It's a bit old-fashioned.

Alan I've got a bed-sitting room.
Jean Have you? What's it like?
Alan It's a bit small.

Three

> # Role play
>
> You want a holiday flat or a house for the summer; or you have a flat or a house to let. Your teacher will give you more information.

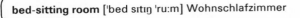

bed-sitting room ['bed sɪtɪŋ 'ruːm] Wohnschlafzimmer

let [let] vermieten

Four

Furniture

Look at the pictures and write the name of each piece of furniture under the right picture.

chair	armchair	coffee table
sofa	television	bookcase
cupboard	chest of drawers	lamp

1 ....

2 ....

3 ....

4 ....

5 ....

6 ....

7 ....

8 ....

9 ....

Five

Penny's bed-sitter

Read this:

''I haven't got a house and I haven't got a flat. I've got a bed-sitting room. It's not a very big room, but it's nice and sunny, and it's very quiet.

   I've got a sofa and two armchairs by a coffee table, and the television's opposite the sofa. I've got a bookcase along one wall, with a lamp on it. The carpet's brown and the walls are a sort of light green. I've got a picture of a lake on one wall, and a chest of drawers under the window. That's all really.

   Oh, and I've got a toilet and a shower in a sort of big cupboard by the door.''

Now look at the picture of the bed-sitter and write the names of the pieces of furniture in the right places.

> **quiet** ['kwaɪət] ruhig
> **opposite** ['ɒpəzɪt] gegenüber
> **bookcase** ['bʊkkeɪs] Bücherschrank, -regal
> **carpet** ['kɑːpɪt] Teppich
> **chest of drawers** ['tʃest əv 'drɔːz] Kommode
> **shower** ['ʃaʊə] Dusche

Six

A new bed-sitter

Draw the furniture in the bed-sitting room.
Put it where you like.

a sofa	a television
a bookcase	a shower
a cupboard	two armchairs
two chairs	a lamp
a coffee table	a chest of drawers
a bed	a toilet

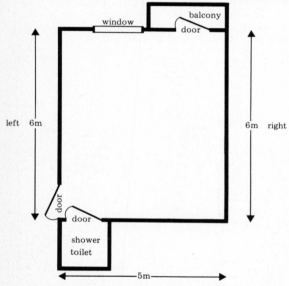

Now tell your teacher where the furniture is,
like this:
"I've got a sofa and a coffee table by the
window, and ...."

Now you can ask your friend "Where's your
coffee table?" Etc.

> **draw** [drɔ:] zeichnen

Seven

Asking the way

Woman Excuse me, where's the theatre, please?
Man It's on the right, near the police station.
Woman Thank you.

Man Excuse me, where's the post office, please?
Woman It's on the left, opposite the Odeon cinema.
Man Thank you.

Now you ask and answer like this about the library,
the restaurant, the Odeon cinema, the toilets,
the police station, the garage and the travel agents.

> **library** ['laɪbrərɪ] Bücherei, Bibliothek
> **garage** ['gærɑ:dʒ] Tankstelle

Eight

Translate these sentences

Translate these sentences into German.
Use idiomatic German.

1 I've got a new flat.
2 It's on the second floor.
3 It's not very big.
4 Where are my books?
5 They're on the table.

Now translate these sentences into English.
Try not to look at the sentences above.

6 Wo ist dein Büro?
7 Es liegt im vierten Stock.
8 Es ist nicht sehr groß.
9 Wo ist meine neue Brille?
10 Sie liegt auf dem Bücherregal.

Nine

Problem

Three couples are having dinner together.
Mr Reynolds is the host.
Mrs Greenbaum is a housewife.
Mrs **Carter** is a bank clerk.
The housewife's husband is a teacher.
The hostess is sitting opposite her husband.
Mr **Carter** is a cook.
The bank clerk is on the host's right.
The housewife is on the host's left.
Her husband is on the hostess' left.
Mr **Carter** is on Mrs Greenbaum's left.

What is Mr Greenbaum's job?

....

Who is sitting on his left?

....

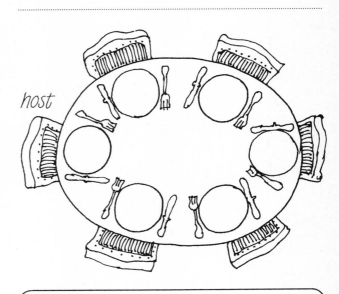

host

| couple ['kʌpl] Paar |
| host [həʊst] Gastgeber |
| hostess ['həʊstɪs] Gastgeberin |

The housing problem

Can you answer these questions?
If you can't, read the text, and try again.

1 How many people live in London?
2 Do they all have a proper home?
3 How many homeless families do you think there are in London – 2,000, 20,000 or 200,000?

4 What is the situation in other big English towns?
5 Can you give three big city housing problems?

....

....

....

About 8 million people live in London. But not all of them have a proper house or flat to live in. About 200,000 families are homeless.

Sometimes the father, mother and children cannot live together; or they all live together in one room without a kitchen or bathroom.

The situation is the same in most of the big towns in Britain, and it is probably the same in all the big cities of the world. Everywhere you find the same three problems: overcrowding, slums and high rents.

housing problem ['haʊzɪŋ 'prɒbləm] Wohnungsproblem
proper ['prɒpə] richtig, ordentlich
probably ['prɒbəblɪ] wahrscheinlich
overcrowding [əʊvə'kraʊdɪŋ] Überbevölkerung
rent [rent] Miete
town planning ['taʊn plænɪŋ] Stadtplanung
not enough [nɒt ɪ'nʌf] nicht genügend
all the same ['ɔːl ðə 'seɪm] trotz(alle)dem

Opinions

What do you think about the town planning in your district?

Robert Mortimer, 52, mechanic
"I think we've got too many blocks of flats and not enough houses."

Marion Ellis, 40, architect
"It's very good. We've got a nice shopping centre and a beautiful park."

Jennifer Plowman, 30, secretary
"I live in the centre of a town in an old block of flats. It's noisy and overcrowded but I like it all the same."

10. He's a nice man

Robert C. Jones, the manager of Universal Services in New York and Linda Burns, the San Francisco manager are coming to London on Tuesday on a business trip. John Austin is looking after them in London, so he asks Mary Hudson about them.

John　Do you know Mr Jones?
Mary　Yes, I do.
John　What's he like?
Mary　Oh, he's nice. I like him.
　　　　He talks a lot, but he's very friendly.
John　How old is he?
Mary　Oh, about fifty-five or sixty, I should think.
John　What about Miss Burns? What's her first name?
Mary　Linda. Oh, she's about thirty-five.
John　What does she look like?
Mary　She's very smart.
John　Is she?
Mary　But I don't like her very much.
John　Why not?
Mary　Well, ... I don't know ...
　　　　She's not my type.
　　　　I just don't like her.
John　Huh! You women are all the same!
Mary　And you men are all the same, too!

manager [ˈmænɪdʒə] Chef, Direktor
know [nəʊ] kennen
friendly [ˈfrendlɪ] freundlich

How to say it

Describing people

1

Do you know	Mr Jones?	Yes.
	Miss Burns?	Yes, I do.
	the Hudsons?	No.
	Brian Hammond?	No, I don't.

● Gr 24, 25 A, 27 B ● Ex 7

Now ask questions like this.

2

What's	John	like?	He's	very nice.	I	like	him.
	he		She's	nice.	I don't		her.
	Mary			all right.			
	she			awful.			
What are	the Hudsons		They're				them.
	they						

● Gr 19 ● Ex 7, 8

Now ask and answer like this.

3 and – but – so – or

Miss Curran is about twenty *and* very attractive.
She lives in London *and* works in Paris.

Bill talks a lot *but* he's very friendly.
He's very old *but* he's very lively.

John is going to look after Mr Jones, *so* he asks
Mary about him.
I start work early tomorrow, *so* I'm going home now.

Carl is about fifty-five *or* sixty.
I think he's a Swede, *or* perhaps he's a Dane.

Now write sentences like these.

Phrases

Practise saying these phrases.

What about...?
Well,...
Why not?
Huh!
...I should think.
...all the same.
(See Ex 1.)

Exercises

One

Pairs

Put the sentences in A with the right sentences in B.

A 1 Cheerio, dear, I'm going to the football match.
   2 I don't think Susan's coming.
   3 How old's Mrs Turner?
   4 Are you going abroad this summer?
   5 What do you think of the new cars this year?

B 1 About eighty, I should think.
   2 Why not?
   3 Huh! You men!
   4 Well, perhaps, if we can.
   5 Oh, they're all the same.

Two

People

A Who's the slim woman with the glasses?
B She's Rita Stern, our secretary.

Now look at the picture of the people who work at Universal Services.
Ask and answer questions about the people with the help of the words.

> **slim** [slɪm] schlank
> **accountant** [əˈkaʊntənt] Buchhalter
> **bald** [bɔːld] kahl, mit Glatze
> **caretaker** [ˈkeəteɪkə] Hauswart, -meister

dark hair	fair hair	beard	glasses	glasses	moustache

Mary Hudson
tours manager

short

John Austin
assistant manager

short

Arthur Goodman
manager

tall

Rita Stern
secretary

slim

Bob Spence
accountant

bald

George Appleby
caretaker

short, fat

Three

Can I help you?

A Can I help you?
B I'm looking for the accountant.
A Oh, that's Mr Spence.
   He's the bald man with the glasses.
B Thank you.

Now look at the picture on p 97 again and make
conversations like this.

look for ['lʊk fə] suchen

Four

Passport, please

Read this passport description.

Family name: JONES
Forename(s):   ROBERT COLUMBUS
Date and place of birth: 4 March 1918 BALTIMORE
Nationality: AMERICAN
Color of hair: GRAY
Color of eyes: BROWN
Height: 175 cms
Special features: MOUSTACHE
Signature: *Robert C. Jones*

Now fill in your own passport description.

Family name: ....

Forename(s): ....

Date and place of birth: ....

Nationality: ....

Colour of hair: ....

Colour of eyes: ....

Height: ....

Special features: ....

Signature: ....

Five

Holiday clothes

Look at this advertisement and choose your own colours, for example:

For him: "I'll have a dark brown suit, a green jacket and grey trousers, and blue jeans and a black sweater."

For her: "I'll have a light blue dress, a red skirt and a white blouse, and white jeans and a yellow sweater.

You can also choose a shirt and tie for him, and a pair of shoes for her.

choose [tʃuːz] wählen

Six

Role play

A person in your family is missing!
Ring the police and give them a
description of the missing person.
Your teacher will give you more
information.

description [dɪ'skrɪpʃn] Beschreibung

Missing person Date: .... Time: ....

Name: .... Tel no. ....

Address: ....

Age: ....

Colour of hair: blonde/brown/dark/black/red

Colour of eyes: blue/brown/green/grey

Height: ....

Build: fat/slim/tall/short

Clothes: ....

Special features: ....

Reported missing by: ....

Result: ....

Seven

What's he like?

A Do you know Eric Goodman?
B No, I don't think so. What's he like?
A Well, he's very nice, but he isn't very lively.

He's very *nice*
but he isn't very *lively*.

| nice |
| friendly |
| interesting |
| lively |
| attractive |
| intelligent |

Now think of a person and talk to a friend about
him or her.
Use the words in the box.

Eight

He–him She–her They–them

Look at these sentences and see how
he, him, she, her, they and *them* are used.

A What do you think of Jean Todd?
B **She**'s very nice. I like **her**.

A What do you think of Edward Cross?
B **He** isn't very friendly. I don't like **him**.

A What do you think of the Richardsons?
B Oh, **they**'re nice. I like **them** very much.

Now fill in the missing words:

John Austin is a nice chap. People like ....
.... works at Universal Services London
Office. Mary Hudson works there too, so John
sees .... every day. .... has the
office opposite John's. Sometimes ....
have lunch together.

   Next week Mr Jones and Miss Burns are
coming to London. .... are coming by
plane, of course. John is going to meet
.... at the airport. Do you think
.... 'll be late? ! And Mary is going to
arrange a programme for ....

Nine

Translate these sentences

Translate these sentences into German.
Use idiomatic German.

1 Do you know Elizabeth James?
2 How old is she?
3 She's about 45, I should think.
4 What's she like?
5 I don't like her very much, actually.

Now translate these sentences into English.
Try not to look at the German sentences.

6 Kennen Sie Mike West?
7 Wie alt ist er?
8 Er ist ungefähr 30, glaube ich.
9 Wie ist er?
10 Eigentlich kann ich ihn nicht sehr gut leiden.

Ten

Make a conversation

Put the words in the right order and make
a conversation.

1	2	3	4	5
Mrs Travers like? What's	but She's very not nice. lively very she's	like don't her. I	she? old is How	or think. sixty should About I fifty-five

A question of lar

An Englishman is sitting in a small restaurant in a one-eyed town in Turkey. He orders a cup of coffee and two chocolate biscuits – in English, of course, because he can't speak Turkish.
An American with a big fat cigar in his mouth is sitting at the next table. He turns round with a smile and says:

"Gee, it sure is great to hear someone speak my language!"

The Englishman looks up and replies,

"Excuse me, sir, I am not speaking *your* language. You are trying to speak mine."

They say that Britain and America are two countries divided by the same language.

~~gu~~age

Right or wrong?

1 The Englishman is in a large town in Turkey.
2 He orders a cup of tea.
3 He speaks very good Turkish.
4 He likes chocolate biscuits.
5 The American is smoking.
6 The American is glad to hear English spoken.
7 The Englishman thinks that the American speaks very good English.
8 Some people think that Englishmen and Americans don't understand each other very well.

> **one-eyed** ['wʌn aɪd] einsam
> **turn round** [tɜːn 'raʊnd] sich umdrehen
> **Gee, it sure is great** ['dʒiː, ɪt 'ʃʊər ɪz 'greɪt] Herrje, das ist ja wirklich prima
> **reply** [rɪ'plaɪ] antworten
> **country** ['kʌntrɪ] Land
> **divided** [dɪ'vaɪdɪd] getrennt, geteilt
> **give it up** ['gɪv ɪt 'ʌp] es aufgeben

Opinions

What do you think about smoking?

Karen Stone, 31, script girl
"I smoke 25 cigarettes a day. I know it's bad for me but I can't give it up."

Harold Cripps, 55, caretaker
"I've given it up many times."

Helen Tanner, 26, journalist
"I don't smoke. I don't think people should smoke at work."

11. What are you do

Mr Jones and Miss Burns are in London now.
It's Friday and John and Mr Jones are in John's office.

John   What are you doing at the weekend, Mr Jones?

Jones   Nothing special. Oh – and please call me Bob.

John   All right, Bob. You see, Monique and me – that's
a French girl I know – we're going to Brighton
at the weekend.
Would you like to come too?

Jones   Well, that's very kind of you, John.
I'd like to very much.

John   What about Miss Burns?
Would she like to come, do you think?

Jones   Well, I don't know. I think she's seeing
some friends in Scotland this weekend.
Shall I give her a call?

John   Yes, do. Use my phone.

Jones   Thanks.
(He rings Miss Burns.)

Jones   No, I'm sorry, she can't.
She *is* seeing some friends in Scotland.

John   Oh, what a pity. Another time, perhaps.
But you'll come, I hope?

Jones   Sure, thanks very much, John, I'd love to.

---

nothing [ˈnʌθɪŋ] nichts
Oh, what a pity! [ˈəʊ ˈwɒt ə ˈpɪtɪ] Ach, wie schade!

---

g at the weekend?

How to say it

Planning; inviting and replying to invitations

1

What	are you is he is she are they	doing	at the weekend?	Nothing special. Let's see.

• Gr 34 • Ex 2, 5

Now ask and answer like this.

2

I'm He's She's We're They're	going to Brighton. going to the country. seeing some friends. going away on business. having a party.	Oh, I see. What a pity!

• Gr 34, 5 • Ex 2, 3, 5

You can answer the questions in 1 like this, too.

3

Would	you he she they	like to come?	Yes, thank you. That's very kind of you. Well, I don't know. I'm sorry, I/we/he/ she/they can't.

• Gr 35 • Ex 3

Ask and answer like this.

4

I'd (I would) We'd He'd She'd They'd	like to very much.

• Gr 35

You can answer the questions in 3 like this, too.

Months

January
February
March
April
May
June
July
August
September
October
November
December

Seasons

spring
summer
autumn
winter

Phrases
Practise saying these phrases.

Nothing special.
Yes, do.
What a pity!
You see, . . .
That's very kind of you.
Another time, perhaps.
. . ., do you think?
I'm sorry, . . .
(See Ex 1.)

Exercises

One

Pairs

Put the sentences in A with the right sentences in B.

A 1 Can I use your phone?
2 I'm going to the theatre today.
   I can get your tickets for you.
3 Can Susan baby-sit for us tomorrow evening?
4 I can't come to the party, I'm working late.
5 What are you doing this evening?

B 1 Nothing special.
2 What a pity! Another time, perhaps.
3 That's very kind of you. Thank you.
4 Yes, please do.
5 No, I'm sorry, she can't.

Two

A diary

This is the Burtons' diary for next week.
Say what they are doing, like this:
They're going to the country on Sunday.
or: On Sunday they're going to the country.
Then ask like this:
What are they doing on . . . day?

May

Sun	7	going to the country
Mon	8	Judith going to her French course
Tue	9	Jim working late
Wed	10	playing badminton
Thu	11	party at the Gardiners'
Fri	12	school meeting
Sat	13	staying at home – watching "South Pacific" on TV

Three

An invitation

Read this dialogue.

Bill is talking to Judith Burton on the phone.

Bill Hullo, Judith. Bill here.
Judith Hullo, Bill. How are you?
Bill Fine, thanks.
   Look, we're having a party on Tuesday.
   Can you and Jim come?
Judith Oh, that's very kind of you.
   Hold on a minute. I'll just ask Jim . . .
   – – –
   I'm sorry, we can't. Jim's working late
   on Tuesday.
Bill What a pity! Oh well. Another time,
   perhaps.
Judith Yes, thanks. Bye-bye.
Bill Bye.

Now *you* invite the Burtons to a party one evening next week, and see if they can come.

Four

Role play

You are having a party.
Phone some friends and invite them to a party.
Your teacher will give you more information.

Five

Your diary

Now you write your diary for next week.

Sun	
Mon	
Tue	
Wed	
Thu	
Fri	
Sat	

Six

A party

The Burtons are going out to a party – at last!
Jim can't find his blue tie...

Put in the missing words: *in – on – by – under*

Jim   Where on earth is my blue tie?

Judith I don't know. Look .... the cupboard.
Jim   It's not there.

Judith Well, look .... the table and

.... the bed.
Jim   No, it's not there, either.
Judith Well, I don't know. You men are
all the same.

Look .... your chest of drawers.
Jim   Which drawer?
Judith I don't know. The top one, perhaps.
Jim   No, it isn't there.

Judith Is it .... the bed, then?
Jim   I don't think so. – No. – Oh!
Judith What?

Jim   It's .... my pocket.
Judith Huh! You men!
Jim   I know – we're all the same.

Seven

Where is it?

Now you write a conversation like the one
in number six.

Ask about a blouse – Where's my blouse?
Or a pair of socks – Where are my socks?
Or something else you can't find.

Eight

Translate these sentences

Translate these sentences into German.
Use idiomatic German.

1 We're having a party on Saturday.
2 Would you like to come?
3 That's very kind of you.
4 But we're going to the country.
5 What a pity! Another time, perhaps.
   In July.

Now translate these sentences into English.
Try not to look at the sentences above.

6 Ich gebe am Dienstag eine Party.
7 Hättest du Lust zu kommen?
8 Das ist sehr nett von dir.
9 Aber ich muß am Montag nach London
   fahren.
10 Wie schade! Ein andermal vielleicht.
   Vielleicht im Juni.

Nine

Problem

Where is the Royal Pavilion?
Look at the map of Brighton below,
and the information under it.
Then try to fill in the missing information.

The Steine [stiːn] Straße in Brighton
market [ˈmɑːkɪt] Markt
hospital [ˈhɒspɪtl] Krankenhaus
corner [ˈkɔːnə] Ecke

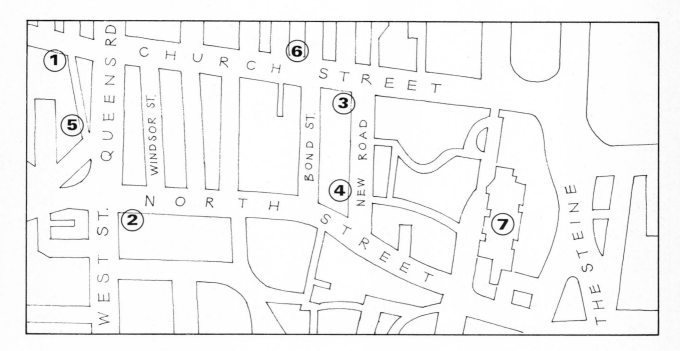

The theatre is in New Road.
Number two is a cinema.
The Royal Pavilion is *not* number one.
The market is in Church Street.
Number five is a Chinese restaurant.
The hospital is at the corner of Queen's Road and Church Street.
There is a church at the corner of New Road and Church Street.

1 The cinema is in ....

2 The Chinese restaurant is in ....

3 The hospital is number ....

4 The theatre is number ....

5 The market is number ....

6 The church is number ....

7 What number is the Royal Pavilion? ....

Brighton by the sea

What do you know about Brighton?

Can you answer these questions?
Answer as many as you can. Then read the text and try to answer all the questions.

1 Is Brighton on the east coast of England?
2 Is it about 40 miles from London?
3 Can you get there by train in an hour?
4 Is there a university at Brighton?
5 What is the most famous building in the town?
6 What brings many foreigners to Brighton?
7 What is the Royal Pavilion now?

Brighton is a big seaside town on the south coast of England. It is about 60 miles south of London, and it only takes an hour to get there by train.

It is full of hotels, restaurants, coffee houses, pubs and shops. But Brighton is also an administrative and a cultural centre. It has a university just outside the town, two technical colleges, several theatres and dozens of schools.

Perhaps the most famous building is the Royal Pavilion. This is now a museum, but in the early 19th century it was the summer palace of King George IV.

All this means that Brighton is a very good holiday centre. In fact many foreigners come to Brighton to study English at one of the many language schools in the town – and to enjoy a typical English holiday by the sea at the same time.

---

famous [ˈfeɪməs] berühmt
foreigner [ˈfɒrɪnə] Fremde(r)
several [ˈsevrəl] mehrere
dozens of [ˈdʌznz əv] Dutzende von

in the 19th century [ɪn də ˈnaɪntiːnθ ˈsentʃərɪ] im 19. Jahrhundert
language school [ˈlæŋgwɪdʒ skuːl] Sprachschule
enjoy [ɪnˈdʒɔɪ] genießen

retired [rɪˈtaɪəd] pensioniert
sailor [ˈseɪlə] Seemann
host [həust] Gastgeber

Opinions

What do you think about parties?

Joan Randall, 42, shop manager
"Parties are all the same. I don't like them."

Stephen Frick, 63, retired sailor
"I think parties are fun."

Irene Thompson, 49, teacher
"Parties are fine for the guests, but they're a lot of work for the hosts."

12. Can I get you an

Mary Hudson is standing at the door of John's office.

Mary I'm just going to the shops.
Can I get you anything?

John Oh, yes please.
Can you get me a packet of cigarettes?

Mary What sort?

John Marlboro, please.

Mary Okay. Anything else?

John No, I don't think so, thanks.
Oh, you're not going to the bank, are you?

Mary No, sorry.

John Never mind, then.
I'm going out to lunch, you see.

At Antonio's Restaurant.
John and Penny are sitting at a table for two.

John Would you like a drink?

Penny No thanks. What's on the menu?

John Er, fried fish, roast beef or ham salad.
And lasagne.

Penny What are you going to have?

John Roast beef, I think. What about you?

hing?

Penny — The same, please.
Do you know that girl over there?

John — No – where?

Penny — Over there. In the corner.
She's waving to you.

John — Oh, er, well, not exactly.

Penny — She's coming over.

John — Oh, my God.

Monique — Hullo, John.

John — Hullo, Monique. Er, this is Penny.
Penny, this is Monique. She's French.

Penny — Hullo.

Monique — Hullo. What is it you English say?
Two's company, three's a crowd?
Goodbye.

anything else [ˈenɪθɪŋ ˈels] noch etwas
never mind [ˈnevə ˈmaɪnd] macht nichts
fried fish [fraɪd ˈfɪʃ] Bratfisch
ham salad [ˈhæm ˈsæləd] Schinkensalat
wave to [ˈweɪv tə] zuwinken
company [ˈkʌmpənɪ] Gesellschaft
crowd [kraʊd] (Menschen-)Menge

"TWO'S COMPANY, THREE'S A CROWD"

How to say it

Asking for something; offering something

1

You're not	going to the bank, going to the shops, going to the post office, going to the chemist's, going to the supermarket,	are you?	Yes. Yes, I am. No. No, I'm not. No, sorry.

Ask and answer questions like this.

• *Gr 27, 34* • *Ex 5*

2

Can I get you	anything? anything else?	No thanks. Yes please. Can you get me . . .

• *Gr 21* • *Ex 5*

3

a box a bottle a packet a kilo	of	matches shampoo cigarettes coffee

• *Gr 17* • *Ex 2, 3, 5*

Ask and answer with the questions and phrases in 2 and 3.

4

Would you like	ham salad or fried fish? roast beef or ham salad? coffee or ice-cream?	Fried fish, Roast beef, Coffee,	please.

Choose your lunch like this.

• *Gr 35* • *Ex 6*

5

Where's	John? Monique?	He's She's	having lunch. sitting over there.
Where are Penny and John?		They're	doing the shopping.

Now ask questions about people you know, like this.

• *Gr 30*

the chemist's [ðə ˈkemɪsts] Apotheke

Phrases

Practise saying these phrases.

I'm just going to . . .
What sort?
Okay.
Anything else?
No, I don't think so.
Never mind.
. . . you see.
. . . this time.
Aha!
Guess!
Well, not exactly.
(See Ex 1.)

Exercises
One

Sentence pairs

Put the sentences in A with the right sentences in B.

A 1 You're not going to the post office, are you?
2 See you tomorrow, then.
3 They haven't got any roast beef.
4 Can you get me some cigarettes, please?
5 Who's going to be our new boss?

B 1 What sort?
2 Guess!
3 Okay.
4 Never mind.
5 No, I'm sorry, I'm not.

Two

Shopping

Write the correct phrase under the pictures:

> a packet of...   a box of...   a bottle of...
> a bar of...   a can of...

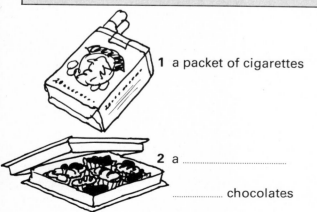

1 a packet of cigarettes

2 a ....
.... chocolates

3 a ....
.... shampoo

4 ....
.... matches

5 ....
.... aspirins

6 ....
.... nuts

7 ....
.... soap

8 ....
.... sherry

9 ....
.... beer

10 ....
.... chocolate

Three

A shopping list

Post office	Two eight-penny stamps
	Three four-penny stamps
Chemist's	A bottle of shampoo
	A bar of soap
	A bottle of aspirins
Paper shop	The local paper
	Three packets of cigarettes
	A box of matches
	A bar of milk chocolate
	A box of chocolates
Supermarket	A packet of corn flakes
	A litre of milk
	A kilo of coffee
	A bottle of sherry
	Two cans of beer
	A packet of nuts
Bank	Cash a cheque for £25

Ask and answer like this:
Where do you get *cigarettes?*
At the *paper shop,* or the *supermarket.*

Four

Your shopping list

Now make your shopping list for the weekend.

Five

Can you get me...

Read these two conversations:

John You're not going to the *bank,* are you?
Jean No, I'm sorry, I'm not.

John You're not going to the *supermarket* are you?
Mary Yes. Can I get you anything?
John Yes please. Can you get me *a litre of milk.*
Mary Okay.
John Thanks.

Now look at your shopping list and have conversations like these with two friends.

Six

At a tea shop

THE BLACK CAT

Tea, per person	10p
Coffee, per person	12p
Milk, per glass	8p
Sandwiches	
Cheese and tomato	25p
Ham	30p
Egg and tomato	25p
Cakes	
Chocolate cake, per portion	15p
Fruit cake, per portion	12p
Danish pastry	16p

Now read this dialogue:

John What are you going to have?
Penny Tea, I think. What about you?
John I'll have the same.
Would you like a sandwich or just a cake?
Penny Um, a Danish pastry would be nice.
Are you going to have anything?
John Yes. A ham sandwich, I think.

(To the waitress)
Two teas, please. And a Danish pastry
and a ham sandwich, please.
And can I have the bill, please.

> cheese [tʃiːz] Käse
> Danish pastry ['deɪnɪʃ 'peɪstrɪ] Blätterteiggebäck

Seven

Role play

You are going out to tea at the Black Cat with a friend.
Your teacher will give you more information.

Eight

Tesco's Supermarket

Here is an advertisement from a supermarket.
Read it, make a shopping list,
and then find out how much your shopping will cost.

pork chop ['pɔːk tʃɒp] Schweinekotelett
butter ['bʌtə] Butter
crisp bread ['krɪsp bred] Knäckebrot
shrimp [ʃrɪmp] Garnele, Krabbe

Nine

Translate these sentences

Translate these sentences into German.
Use idiomatic German.

 1 I'm just going to the shops.
 2 Can I get you anything?
 3 No, thanks. I don't think so.
 4 Oh, you're not going to the bank, are you?
 5 No, sorry.

Now translate these sentences into idiomatic English. Try not to look at the sentences above.

 6 Ich gehe mal einkaufen.
 7 Kann ich dir was mitbringen?
 8 Danke, nein. Ich glaube nicht.
 9 Du gehst nicht etwa zur Post?
10 Leider nein.

Tesco's Supermarket

Fruit salad 23p
Orange juice 38p
Tomato soup 15p
Instant coffee 46p
Beer 19p
Sugar 14p per kilo

Eggs 46p per dozen
Butter 30p per 1/2 kilo
Cheddar cheese 78p per 1/2 kilo
Potatoes 6p per kilo
Apples 40p per kilo

Bananas 32p per kilo
Pork chop 24p
Shrimps 20p per hecto
White bread 15p
Crisp bread 20p
Chocolate biscuits 28p

Silly stories

Do you know the story about... Try to remember these stories,
and then tell them to a friend.

There's a fly

Man Waiter, there's a fly in my soup.
Waiter It's all right, sir. He's dead.

Man Waiter, there's a fly in my soup.
Waiter Don't worry, sir. They don't drink much.

Man Waiter, there's a fly in my soup.
Waiter Don't worry, sir. There's no extra charge.

Man Waiter, there's a fly in my soup.
Waiter Don't worry, sir. Flies can swim.

Man Waiter, there's a fly in my soup.
Waiter Shh, sir. Not so loud,
or all the other guests will want one.

Man Waiter, there's a fly in my soup.
Waiter Don't worry, sir.
The spider on the bread will get him.

Tiger steak

Do you know the one about the tiger steak?

A man goes into a restaurant and asks for the menu. When the waiter gives it to him, he is very surprised. All the food is very funny: Elephant's Ear Soup, Roast Crocodile, Fried Flies Feet and so on. Of course, he thinks it is all a joke.

"I'll have the tiger steak, please," he says to the waiter with a smile.

"Yes, sir," the waiter says, without a smile.

"Would you like it rare, medium or well-done?"

"Er, oh, medium, please," the man says. And five minutes later the waiter is back with a beautiful steak on a plate.

"Your tiger steak, sir."

"That isn't a tiger steak!" the man says. "You must be joking!"

"No, sir. We never joke. Come into the kitchen and see."

So the man goes into the kitchen and there, on the table, he sees a tiger, with one steak cut out of its side. The man is very surprised — and goes back and eats his tiger steak. Then he looks at the menu again. And he reads under Sweets: Mermaid's Tail on Toast.

"Aha!" he says to himself. "That can't be right. Waiter!"

"Sir?"

"I'll have the Mermaid's Tail on Toast, please."

"One Mermaid's Tail on Toast. Yes, sir," the waiter says, without any surprise, and goes out into the kitchen. The man waits but the waiter doesn't come back for a long time. At last he comes in; he looks very worried.

"Sir, I am terribly sorry. This has never happened before! Never. We can't give you Mermaid's Tail on Toast. We haven't got any bread."

---

worry [ˈwʌrɪ] sich Sorgen machen
charge [tʃɑːdʒ] Kosten
loud [laʊd] laut
spider [ˈspaɪdə] Spinne
fried flies feet [ˈfraɪd ˈflaɪz] gebratene Fliegenfüße
joke [dʒəʊk] Witz, Scherz
rare [reə] blutig
medium [ˈmiːdjəm] noch saftig
well-done [welˈdʌn] (gut) durchgebraten
mermaid's tail [ˈmɜːmeɪdz teɪl] Seejungfrauenschwanz
toast [təʊst] Toast
bachelor [ˈbætʃələ] Junggeselle

Opinions

How do you do your shopping?

James Gibson, 39, bachelor
"I do all my shopping at the supermarket."

Lynne Moore, 72, artist
"You get better service in the small shops."

Rosemary Peters, 44, factory worker
"We try to do all the shopping on Saturday morning."

13. Would you like

John is having coffee with Linda Burns in the cafeteria at the office. Mary Hudson comes in with Peter Lord, a new assistant.

Mary   Hullo. This is our new assistant, Peter Lord.
John   Hullo.
Linda   Hullo.
Mary   This is Linda Burns from the San Francisco office.
And this is John Austin. He works here.
Peter   Hullo.
John   Sit down.
Peter   Thanks.

Mary   Would you like some coffee?
Peter   Yes please. (She gives him a cup.)
Thank you.
Mary   Sugar?
Peter   No thanks.
John   Where's your office, Peter?
Peter   On the second floor, opposite yours.
John   Oh, yes? What's it like?
Peter   It's fine, thanks.
John   Good.

Mary   What are you doing at the weekend, Linda?
Linda   Oh, I'm going back to San Francisco, I'm afraid.
John   Oh dear! When are you going?
Linda   On Saturday morning. At 10.
John   Oh, I'm going to the airport on Saturday morning.
Can I give you a lift?
Linda   That's very kind of you. Thanks very much.
John   I'll pick you up about 8.30 at your hotel. Okay?
Linda   Fine.

some coffee?

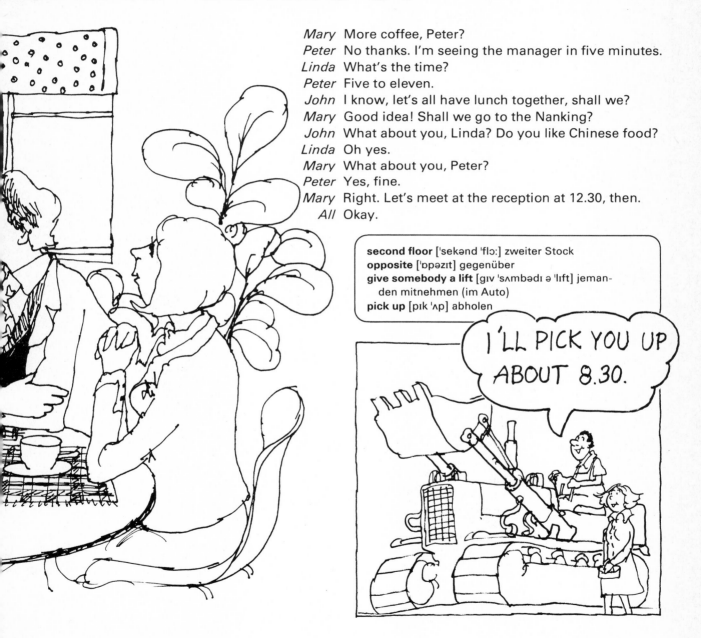

Mary More coffee, Peter?

Peter No thanks. I'm seeing the manager in five minutes.

Linda What's the time?

Peter Five to eleven.

John I know, let's all have lunch together, shall we?

Mary Good idea! Shall we go to the Nanking?

John What about you, Linda? Do you like Chinese food?

Linda Oh yes.

Mary What about you, Peter?

Peter Yes, fine.

Mary Right. Let's meet at the reception at 12.30, then.

All Okay.

second floor ['sekənd 'flɔː] zweiter Stock
opposite ['ɒpəzɪt] gegenüber
give somebody a lift [gɪv 'sʌmbədɪ ə 'lɪft] jemanden mitnehmen (im Auto)
pick up [pɪk 'ʌp] abholen

I'LL PICK YOU UP ABOUT 8.30.

How to say it

Time, place and method

AT	at the weekend at 10 o'clock
ON	on Saturday on Monday morning on (the) 10th (of) January

PLACE

AT	at the office at the airport at the reception at the cinema
IN	in London in Baker Street in the street in the cafeteria in the corner
TO	Go to Oxford to the country to Sweden
WITH	Come with me Have lunch with John
FROM	I'm from Manchester from Universal Services
ON	on the second floor on the left on the right on the floor on the wall
NEAR	near the office near the railway station

OPPOSITE	opposite the post office opposite Peter Lord
BESIDE	beside the bookcase beside Linda Burns
BY	by the door by the window
BEHIND	behind the desk behind you
IN FRONT OF	in front of the window in front of you
UNDER	under the clock under the window
OVER	over the table over the door over there
ROUND	round the table

METHOD

BY	I'm going by train by bus by air by boat

Phrases

Practise saying these phrases.

Good!   Oh dear!
Fine!   Right!

Exercises
One

The cafeteria

Look at the picture and the numbers on some of the things in the picture.
Write the word by the right number below.

1 ....
2 ....
3 ....
4 ....
5 ....
6 ....
7 ....
8 ....
9 ....
10 ....

an ashtray	a plant
the bin	the radiator
the counter	the trays
the fruit machines	the lamp
the map	the clock

ashtray [ˈæʃtreɪ] Aschenbecher
bin [bɪn] Abfallkorb, -eimer
counter [ˈkaʊntə] Theke
fruit machine [ˈfruːt məʃiːn] Spielautomat
radiator [ˈreɪdɪeɪtə] Heizkörper
tray [treɪ] Tablett

Two

Missing words

Look at the picture of the cafeteria again and read the questions below.
Then answer the questions; fill in the missing words:
with − in − opposite − beside − by − on − under − over − behind.

1 Where's John?

He's .... the cafeteria.

2 Where's Mary?

She's having coffee .... John.

3 Where's Peter?

.... Mary and John .... the cafeteria.

4 Which one is John?

He's sitting .... Linda. O .... Mary.

5 Yes, but which one is Mary?

She's standing b .... Peter.

6 Are they sitting at the table

by the fruit machines?

No, they're .... the window.

7 Where are the trays?

They're .... the counter.

8 Where's the coffee?

.... the counter.

9 Where's the bin?

.... the corner, ... the radiator.

10 Can you see an ashtray anywhere?

Yes, ... there, ... the table ....

the fruit machines.

11 "Where's the map?" John asks.

"................................ the wall .... the counter,"

Mary answers.

12 "Is there a clock here?" Peter asks.

"Yes, ... the door .... you," Linda

answers.

Three

Look and remember

Work with a friend.
One of you looks at the picture and asks questions,
like the questions in Exercise Two.
The other person closes his or her book and tries
to remember, and answers the questions.

Four

What are you doing at the weekend?

Here is a list of "fun" activities, and a list of famous people.
You are going to spend the weekend with one of them!

have dinner with	Björn Borg
have lunch with	Ingrid Bergman
go to the theatre with	Princess Anne
go to a night club with	Sammy Davis jr
play tennis with	Brigitte Bardot
play poker with	Robert Redford
go for a walk in the country with	Paul McCartney
go away on holiday with	Gunther Sachs
go sailing with	Jacqueline Kennedy Onassis
play golf with	Indira Gandhi
give German lessons to	Prince Philip

Plan your weekend like this:
"I'm *having lunch with Ingrid Bergman* on *Saturday* at *12* o'clock." etc.

You can answer:
"Have a nice time!"
or
"Be careful!"
Plan lots of activities for the weekend.

Five

A real weekend

Write down your real plans for this weekend.

Six

Role play

Have a party!
Use your English!
Your teacher will give you more information.

Opinions

What do you think of this book?

Grammatik

Substantiv

Grammatische Ausdrücke

Substantive sind Bezeichnungen für Personen, Tiere, Gegenstände, Abstrakta usw. In der Regel kann man *ein, das* oder *mehrere* vor das Substantiv setzen, z. B. *ein Stuhl, das Problem, mehrere Lampen.*

Artikel

Ein, eine nennt man den **unbestimmten Artikel,** im Englischen *a* oder *an.*
Der, die, das ist der **bestimmte Artikel,** im Englischen immer *the.*
Im Englischen werden die Substantive also nicht nach Geschlecht unterschieden: *ein/der Mann, eine/die Frau, ein/das Haus = a/the man, a/the woman, a/the house.*

Singular und Plural

Singular bedeutet Einzahl und *Plural* Mehrzahl, z. B. *eine Lampe* (Singular), *mehrere Lampen* (Plural). Im Deutschen bildet man den Plural meist durch Anhängen von Nachsilben *(Junge-n)*, mit Umlaut *(Buch — Bücher)*, manchmal haben Singular und Plural die gleiche Form *(der Keller — die Keller)*. Im Englischen wird der Plural der meisten Substantive durch Anhängen von *-s* gebildet, z. B. *boy — boys.* Auch hier bleibt der bestimmte Artikel *the: the boy — the boys*
der Junge — *die* Jungen

Unbestimmter Artikel

1   a — an

a secretary [ə 'sekrətrı]	eine Sekretärin	● Der unbestimmte Artikel heißt
a nurse [ə 'nɜːs]	eine Krankenschwester	**a** [ə] vor Konsonanten und
an engineer [ən endʒɪ'nɪə]	ein Ingenieur	**an** [ən] vor Vokalen.
an office [ən 'ɒfɪs]	ein Büro	

2   I'm a secretary

I'm a secretary.	Ich bin Sekretärin.	● Im Englischen muß der unbestimmte
He's an engineer.	Er ist Ingenieur.	Artikel stehen, wenn man jemandes Be-
Are you a nurse?	Sind Sie Krankenschwester?	ruf angibt.
Alan is a shop assistant.	Alan ist Verkäufer.	

3   Can you drive a car?

Can you drive a car?	Kannst du Auto fahren?	● Im Englischen steht der unbestimm-
Can you give me a light, please?	Können Sie mir bitte Feuer geben?	te Artikel in manchen Fällen, wo er im Deutschen fehlt.

4 £10 a day

How much is it to hire a car? — About £10 a day. He works forty hours a week.	Was kostet es, ein Auto zu mieten? — 10 Pfund pro Tag. Er arbeitet 40 Stunden in der Woche.	● In Ausdrücken wie ,,10 Pfund pro Tag'' und ,,40 Stunden in der Woche'' verwendet das Englische den unbestimmten Artikel.

5 What a . . .!

What a pity! What a lovely day!	Wie schade. Was für ein schöner Tag!	● Der unbestimmte Artikel wird in Ausdrücken nach *What* . . . verwendet.

Bestimmter Artikel

6 the

the secretary [ðə ˈsekrətrɪ] the nurses [ðə ˈnɜːsɪz] the engineer [ðɪ endʒɪˈnɪə] the office [ðɪ ˈɒfɪs] the London office [ðə ˈlʌndən ˈɒfɪs]	die Sekretärin die Krankenschwestern der Ingenieur das Büro das Londoner Büro	● Der bestimmte Artikel lautet *the* im Singular und Plural. *The* wird ausgesprochen: [ðə] vor Konsonanten, [ðɪ] vor Vokalen.

7 The Palladium

Would you like to go the Palladium? There's a Mozart concert at the Albert Hall. Have you seen the film at the Academy?	Möchtest du ins Palladium gehen? Es gibt ein Mozart-Konzert in der Albert Hall. Hast du den Film in der Akademie gesehen?	● Namen von Theatern, Kinos und Hotels haben den bestimmten Artikel.

8 The Petersens

The Petersens fill in landing cards at London Airport. The United States.	Die Petersens füllen Einreisekarten auf dem Londoner Flughafen aus. Die Vereinigten Staaten.	● Namen im Plural haben den bestimmten Artikel.

9 On the right

The toilet is upstairs on the right. Put the chair in the room on the left.	Die Toilette ist oben auf der rechten Seite. Stell den Stuhl im Zimmer auf die linke Seite.	● Der bestimmte Artikel wird in Ausdrücken mit *right* und *left* verwendet.

10 Play the piano

Mrs Black plays the piano. She doesn't play the guitar.	Frau Black spielt Klavier. Sie spielt nicht Gitarre.	● Der bestimmte Artikel steht vor Musikinstrumenten (nach *play*).

11 Go to the theatre

Shall we go to the theatre? Would you like to go to the cinema?	Wollen wir ins Theater gehen? Möchtest du ins Kino gehen?	● Der bestimmte Artikel steht auch in Ausdrücken wie „ins Theater, Kino gehen". Vgl. aber *watch television*.

Pluralbildung

12 Plural mit -s

Singular	Plural
book [bʊk]	books [bʊks]
month [mʌnθ]	months [mʌnθs]
pub [pʌb]	pubs [pʌbz]
train [treɪn]	trains [treɪnz]
boy [bɔɪ]	boys [bɔɪz]

● Die meisten englischen Substantive bilden den Plural durch Anhängen von -s. Es wird ausgesprochen: stimmlos [s] nach stimmlosen Konsonanten; stimmhaft [z] nach stimmhaften Konsonanten sowie allen Vokalen und Diphthongen. (Siehe S. 139/140)

13 Plural mit -es

Singular	Plural
glass [glɑːs]	glasses ['glɑːsɪz]
coach [kəʊtʃ]	coaches ['kəʊtʃɪz]
sandwich ['sænwɪdʒ]	sandwiches ['sænwɪdʒɪz]
sentence ['sentəns]	sentences ['sentənsɪz]
phrase [freɪz]	phrases ['freɪzɪz]
garage ['gærɑːdʒ]	garages ['gærɑːdʒɪz]

● Endet das Substantiv auf einen Zischlaut [s, z, ʃ, ʒ], wird der Plural durch Anhängen von -es gebildet, das [ɪz] ausgesprochen wird.
● Endet ein Substantiv auf Zischlaut + stummes -e, wird im Plural einfach -s angehängt, ausgesprochen [ɪz].

14 Schreibungsänderungen

Singular	Plural
party ['pɑːtɪ]	parties ['pɑːtɪz]
country ['kʌntrɪ]	countries ['kʌntrɪz]
play [pleɪ]	plays [pleɪz]
boy [bɔɪ]	boys [bɔɪz]

● Substantive, die im Singular auf Konsonant + -y enden, werden im Plural -ies geschrieben.
● Nach Vokalen bleibt -y erhalten.

15 Unregelmäßige Pluralbildung

Singular	Plural
man [mæn]	men [men]
woman ['wʊmən]	women ['wɪmɪn]
child [tʃaɪld]	children ['tʃɪldrən]

● Einige wenige Substantive bilden im Englischen den Plural unregelmäßig.

Genitiv

16 John's card

Dirty Dick's [dɪks] pub. John's [dʒɒnz] card. My girl friend's [frendz] photo. George's ['dʒɔːdʒɪz] car.	Dirty Dicks Pub. Johns Visitenkarte. Das Photo meiner Freundin. Georgs Auto.	● Der Genitiv (Wes-Fall) wird im Englischen mit **'s** (Apostroph + *s*) gebildet, ausgesprochen wie das Plural-*s*: stimmlos [s] nach stimmlosen Lauten, stimmhaft [z] nach stimmhaften Lauten, [ɪz] nach Zischlauten (s. § 12 + 13).

17 A box of matches

A box of matches ['mætʃɪz] A bottle of shampoo [ʃæm'puː] A packet of cigarettes [sɪgə'rets]	Eine Schachtel Streichhölzer Eine Flasche Haarwaschmittel Eine Schachtel Zigaretten	● Wörter zur Bezeichnung von Menge oder Anzahl stehen im Englischen mit *of*.

Zahlwörter

18 Grundzahlen   Ordnungszahlen

Grundzahlen	Ordnungszahlen	
0 **nought** [nɔːt]	**the first** [fɜːst]	1st
1 **one** [wʌn]	**the second** ['sekənd]	2nd
2 **two** [tuː]	**the third** [θɜːd]	3rd
3 **three** [θriː]	**the fourth** [fɔːθ]	4th
4 **four** [fɔː]	**the fifth** [fɪfθ]	5th
5 **five** [faɪv]	**the sixth** [sɪksθ]	6th
6 **six** [sɪks]	**the seventh** ['sevnθ]	7th
7 **seven** ['sevn]	**the eighth** [eɪtθ]	8th
8 **eight** [eɪt]	**the ninth** [naɪnθ]	9th
9 **nine** [naɪn]	**the tenth** [tenθ]	10th
10 **ten** [ten]	**the eleventh** [ɪ'levnθ]	11th
11 **eleven** [ɪ'levn]	**the twelfth** [twelfθ]	12th
12 **twelve** [twelv]	**the thirteenth** [θɜː'tiːnθ]	13th
13 **thirteen** [θɜː'tiːn]	**the fourteenth** [fɔː'tiːnθ]	14th
14 **fourteen** [fɔː'tiːn]	**the fifteenth** [fɪf'tiːnθ]	15th
15 **fifteen** [fɪf'tiːn]	**the sixteenth** [sɪks'tiːnθ]	16th
16 **sixteen** [sɪks'tiːn]	**the seventeenth** [sevn'tiːnθ]	17th
17 **seventeen** [sevn'tiːn]	**the eighteenth** [eɪ'tiːnθ]	18th
18 **eighteen** [eɪ'tiːn]	**the nineteenth** [naɪn'tiːnθ]	19th
19 **nineteen** [naɪn'tiːn]	**the twentieth** ['twentɪθ]	20th
20 **twenty** ['twentɪ]	**the twenty-first** ['twentɪ'fɜːst]	21st
21 **twenty-one** ['twentɪ'wʌn]	**the twenty-second** ['twentɪ'sekənd]	22nd
22 **twenty-two** ['twentɪ'tuː]	**the thirtieth** ['θɜːtɪɪθ]	30th
30 **thirty** ['θɜːtɪ]	**the fortieth** ['fɔːtɪɪθ]	40th
40 **forty** ['fɔːtɪ]	**the fiftieth** ['fɪftɪɪθ]	50th
50 **fifty** ['fɪftɪ]	**the sixtieth** ['sɪkstɪɪθ]	60th
60 **sixty** ['sɪkstɪ]	**the seventieth** ['sevntɪɪθ]	70th
70 **seventy** ['sevntɪ]	**the eightieth** ['eɪtɪɪθ]	80th
80 **eighty** ['eɪtɪ]	**the ninetieth** ['naɪntɪɪθ]	90th
90 **ninety** ['naɪntɪ]	**the hundreth** ['hʌndrədθ]	100th
100 **a/one hundred** ['hʌndrəd]	**the hundred and first**	101st
101 **a/one hundred and one**		

156	a/one hundred and fifty-six			1,000	a/one thousand ['θaʊznd]	
200	two hundred			4,327	four thousand three hundred and twenty-seven	
468	four hundred and sixty-eight			1,000,000	a/one million ['mɪljən]	

Zur Beachtung:

1 Im Englischen steht *a* oder *one* vor *hundred, thousand* und *million. A hundred years* hundert Jahre, *a thousand men* tausend Mann.

2 Ein Komma setzt man zur Kennzeichnung der Tausender oder Millionen: 4,372,540.

3 Zehner und Einer werden durch Bindestrich verbunden: *thirty-six.*

4 Nach Hunderten und höheren Zahlen steht *and* vor folgenden Zehnern (oder Einern, wenn Zehner fehlen): *Four hundred and twelve, two thousand and nine.*

5 Jahreszahlen liest man folgendermaßen: 1632 = *sixteen thirty-two,* 1980 = *nineteen eighty,* 1806 = *eighteen o* [əʊ] *six.*

6 Das Datum wird geschrieben und ausgesprochen:
1st May ⎫ *the first of May*
1 May ⎬
May 1 ⎭ *May the first*

7 Telefonnummern werden folgendermaßen ausgesprochen: 66 04 30 = *double six - o* [əʊ] *four - three o.*

Pronomen

Grammatische Ausdrücke

Pronomen sind Wörter, die andere Wörter (meist Substantive) ersetzen, z. B. *der Mann — er, die Frau — sie, das Auto — es.*

Personalpronomen sind *ich, du, er, sie, es, wir, ihr, sie, Sie.*

Possesivpronomen drücken den Besitz aus, z. B. *mein, dein, sein, unser, euer, ihr, Ihr.*

Unbestimmte Pronomen beziehen sich nicht auf bestimmte Personen oder Sachen, z. B. *niemand, jemand.*

19 Personalpronomen

Singular						
Singular	1	**I** [aɪ]	ich	**me** [mi:]	mir, mich	● Das englische *you* bezeichnet *du, Sie* und *ihr.*
	2	**you** [ju:]	du, Sie	**you** [ju:]	dir, dich	● Im Unterschied zum Deutschen *(der Baum = er, die Blume = sie)* werden im Englischen alle Substantive mit *it* bezeichnet *(the tree = it, the flower = it).*
	3	**he** [hi:]	er	**him** [hɪm]	ihm, ihn	
		she [ʃi:]	sie	**her** [hɜ:]	ihr, sie	
		it [ɪt]	es	**it** [ɪt]	ihm, es	
Plural	1	**we** [wi:]	wir	**us** [ʌs]	uns	
	2	**you** [ju:]	ihr	**you** [ju:]	euch	
	3	**they** [ðeɪ]	sie	**them** [ðem]	ihnen, sie	

What's Mr Jones like?
— He's nice. I like him.
What do you think of Miss Cross?
— She's not very friendly,
  I don't like her.
	Wie ist Mr Jones?
	— Er ist nett, ich mag ihn.
	Was halten Sie von Miss Cross?
	— Sie ist nicht sehr freundlich,
	  ich mag sie nicht.
		● *He/him* bezeichnen männliche Personen, *she/her* weibliche Personen. Also auch *the girl = she* (vgl. dt. *das Mädchen = es*).

20 Possessivpronomen

Singular	1	**my** [maɪ]	mein, meine, mein	● Das Englische verwendet das gleiche Wort *your* für *dein, Ihr, euer.*
	2	**your** [jɔ:]	dein, deine, dein Ihr, Ihre, Ihr	
	3	**his** [hɪz] **her** [hɜ:] **its** [ɪts]	sein, seine, sein ihr, ihre, ihr sein, seine, sein	
Plural	1	**our** ['aʊə]	unser, unsere, unser	
	2	**your** [jɔ:]	euer, eure, euer	
	3	**their** [ðeə]	ihr, ihre, ihr	

Where's my passport? Your ticket is over there. Where's her ticket? Has he paid for his ticket?	Wo ist mein Paß? Deine/Ihre/Eure Fahrkarte ist dort. Wo ist ihre Eintrittskarte? Hat er seine Karte bezahlt?	Die Form des Possessivpronomens ist im Englischen für alle Personen und im Singular und Plural gleich: vgl. dt. mein Paß, dein*e* Fahrkarte, ihr*e* Eintrittskarten.

21 Something — anything

Can I get you anything? I don't want anything else. Let's have something to eat now. I'd like something else. Would you like something to eat?	Kann ich dir was mitbringen? Ich möchte nichts weiter. Laß uns etwas essen. Ich möchte etwas anderes. Möchtest du etwas zu essen?	● *Anything* wird in Fragen und verneinten Sätzen verwendet. ● *Something* steht in Sätzen, die weder fragend noch verneint sind. ● *Something* wird auch verwendet, wenn man etwas anbietet.

Verb

Grammatische Ausdrücke

Verben sind Wörter, die beschreiben, was jemand tut oder was geschieht, z. B. *arbeiten, regnen*.
Die Verben werden in Hauptverben und Hilfsverben eingeteilt.

Hilfsverben sind z. B. *be, have, can, will, would, shall, should, must, do.* Sie stehen im allgemeinen zusammen mit einem
Hauptverb, z. B. *I must go now. Would you like a drink? Shall we go to the cinema? Does she like music?*

Präsens (Gegenwart) ist eine Zeitform der Verben, die die jetzige Zeit bezeichnet, z. B. *ich wohne in Stuttgart.*

Hilfsverben

22   Be (am — is — are)

to be = sein. Das Verb *be* hat im Präsens die folgenden Formen.

		Bejahend	Kurzform	Verneint	Kurzform
		ich bin		ich bin nicht	
Singular	1	I am	I'm	I am not	I'm not
	2	you are	you're	you are not	you're not, you aren't
	3	he she it } is	he's she's it's	he she it } is not	he's not, he isn't
Plural	1	we	we're	we	we're not,
	2	you } are	you're	you } are not	we aren't
	3	they	they're	they	

● Die Kurzformen werden im gesprochenen Englisch und in der ungezwungenen Schriftsprache verwendet (z. B. in privaten Briefen).

Sorry I'm late!	Entschuldigen Sie, daß ich zu spät komme.
John is at London Airport.	John ist auf dem Londoner Flughafen.
Excuse me, are you Mr Petersen?	Entschuldigen Sie, sind Sie Herr Petersen?
Here's (Here is) my card.	Hier ist meine Visitenkarte.
They aren't married.	Sie sind nicht verheiratet.

23 Have

to have = haben. Das Verb *have* hat im Präsens die folgenden Formen.

Bejahend		Kurzform	Verneint (Kurzform)	
1	I	I've	I	
2	you } have	you've	you } haven't got	
3	he	he's	he	
	she } has	she's	she } hasn't got	
	it	it's } got	it	
1	we	we've	we	
2	you } have	you've	you } haven't got	
3	they	they've	they	

● *He's* kann die Kurzform von *he has* und *he is* sein.

● In der Bedeutung „besitzen" wird häufig *got* nach *have/has* hinzugefügt.

I've got a new car.	Ich habe ein neues Auto.	
She's got a new boy friend.	Sie hat einen neuen Freund.	
Have you got the ticket?	Hast du die Fahrkarte?	

● In Sätzen wie *I've got a car* hat *got* keine Entsprechung im Deutschen: Ich habe ein Auto.

24 Do

to do als Hauptverb = tun, machen, z. B. *I never do my homework.*
als Hilfsverb in Fragen und verneinten Sätzen = keine Entsprechung im Deutschen.

Das Verb *do* hat im Präsens die folgenden Formen.

Fragend		Verneint	
1	Do { I?	I	
2	{ you?	You } do not/don't.	
3	Does { he? she? it?	He She It } does not/doesn't.	
1	Do { we?	We	
2	{ you?	You } do not/don't.	
3	{ they?	They	

25 A. Fragen mit do

Do you like sport?	Mögen Sie Sport?	
Does Mary like her work?	Liebt Mary ihre Arbeit?	
How does he know?	Woher weiß er das?	
What do you do in your spare time?	Was machst du in deiner Freizeit?	

● In Fragen muß *do* oder *does* stehen, wenn kein anderes Hilfsverb vorkommt. Vor *do/does* kann noch ein Fragewort stehen. Auch das Verb *do* wird mit *do* umschrieben.

B. Fragen ohne do

Can you come?	Kannst du kommen?	
Must you go?	Mußt du gehen?	
Are you Swedish?	Sind Sie Schwede/Schwedin?	

● Kommt ein anderes Hilfsverb vor, entfällt die Umschreibung mit *do*.

26 **A. Verneinungen mit do**

I don't smoke.	Ich rauche nicht.	● In Verneinungen (Sätzen mit dem
Ann doesn't live here.	Ann wohnt nicht hier.	Wort *not* = nicht) muß *do* oder *does*
Penny doesn't live here, either.	Penny wohnt auch nicht hier.	stehen, wenn kein anderes Hilfsverb vorkommt.

B. Verneinungen ohne do

I can't come tomorrow.	Ich kann morgen nicht kommen.	● Kommt ein anderes Hilfsverb vor,
He isn't at home.	Er ist nicht zu Hause.	entfällt die Umschreibung mit *do*.
She hasn't got a car.	Sie hat kein Auto.	Ebenso wenn ein anderes Verneinungs-
I never work on Sundays.	Sonntags arbeite ich nie.	wort vorkommt, z. B. *never*.

27 **A. Bestätigungsfragen (question tags)**

Nice today, isn't it?	Schön heute, nicht (wahr)?	● Dieser Fragetyp ist im Englischen
You're not going to the bank, are you?	Du gehst nicht zufällig zur Bank?	recht häufig. Im Deutschen wird hier meist „nicht (wahr)?" verwendet.
You can drive a car, can't you?	Du kannst doch Auto fahren, nicht wahr?	Nach einem bejahten Satz ist die Bestätigungsfrage verneint, nach einem
You can't drive a car, can you?	Du kannst doch nicht Auto fahren, oder (doch)?	verneinten Aussagesatz ist sie bejaht. Enthält der Aussagesatz kein Hilfsverb,
You play the guitar, don't you?	Du spielst doch Gitarre, nicht wahr?	so treten *do/does* ein.

B. Kurzantworten

It's nice today. — Yes, it is.	Es ist schön heute. — Ja.	● Antworten mit *yes* oder *no* werden
Are you Mr Petersen? — No, I'm not.	Sind Sie Herr Petersen? — Nein (ich bin es nicht).	im Englischen meist durch einen Kurzsatz ergänzt. Die Kurzantwort greift
Do you like sport? — No, I don't.	Lieben Sie Sport? — Nein.	das Hilfsverb der vorangehenden Frage
Does John like his work? — Yes, he does. [dʌz]	Liebt John seine Arbeit? — Ja.	wieder auf, das Subjekt erscheint als Personalpronomen. Bei den bejahten
Is your flat in Baker Street? — Yes, it is. [ɪz]	Liegt Ihre Wohnung in der Baker Street? — Ja.	Hilfsverben wird die betonte Vollform gesprochen.
You're not going to the bank, are you? — Yes, I am. [æm]	Du gehst nicht zufällig zur Bank? — Doch, ja.	

C. Rückfragen

I'm a secretary. — Are you?	Ich bin Sekretärin. — Wirklich?	● Rückfragen werden aus einem (dem
He's English. — Is he?	Er ist Engländer. — Tatsächlich?	Aussagesatz entsprechenden) Hilfsverb
I'm coming on Tuesday. — Are you?	Ich komme Dienstag. — Ja?	und einem Personalpronomen gebildet.
I don't like football. — Don't you?	Ich mag Fußball nicht. — Wirklich nicht?	Diese Rückfragen sind oft keine echten Fragen, auf die eine Antwort erwartet
I've got a new flat. — Have you?	Ich habe eine neue Wohnung. — Tatsächlich?	wird. Sie drücken meist nur das Interesse an dem vorher Gesagten aus.

Hauptverben

28 Work

to work = arbeiten. Das Verb *work* hat im Präsens die folgenden Formen.

Singular					Plural			
1	I	} work	**3**	he	**1**	we	} work	
2	you			she } works	**2**	you		
				it	**3**	they		

John/He works at Universal Services. John and Mary/They work there. This bus/It stops at Waterloo.	John/Er arbeitet bei *Universal Services*. John und Mary/Sie arbeiten dort. Dieser Bus/Er hält am Waterloo-Bahnhof.	● In der 3. Person Singular wird **-s** an das Verb angehängt. D. h. bei *he, she, it* oder bei Wörtern, die man dadurch ersetzen kann, wie *John, Mary, bus.*

29 Working

Eine sehr häufige Verbform ist im Englischen die *ing-form*, die etwa der deutschen Verbform auf *-end* entspricht, z. B. *folgend, kommend.*	● Die *ing-form* wird gebildet, indem man *-ing* an die Grundform des Verbs anhängt.

Schreibungsänderungen

smoke — smoking sit — sitting	live — living stop — stopping	● Stummes *-e* vor *-ing* entfällt. ● Endkonsonanten werden vor *-ing* verdoppelt, wenn der vorhergehende Vokal kurz und betont ist.
Aber: wait — waiting (Vokal nicht kurz) open — opening (Vokal nicht betont)		

30 I'm working

I'm You're He's We're } working. You're They're	Ich arbeite, bin gerade beim Arbeiten.	● Die Verlaufsform *(Continuous Form)* gibt an, was gerade im Augenblick geschieht. Das *Present Continuous* wird gebildet mit *am, is, are* + *ing-form.*

Penny is sitting over there. She's waving to you. They're doing the shopping.	Penny sitzt dort drüben. Sie winkt dir zu. Sie machen gerade ihre Einkäufe.

Man vergleiche:

Einfaches Präsens *(Simple Present)* Jenny plays the piano.	Jenny spielt Klavier (= kann spielen, spielt gewöhnlich).	● Wiederholte Handlung oder Gewohnheit.
Verlaufsform *(Present Continuous)* Jenny is playing the piano.	Jenny spielt Klavier (= ist gerade mit dem Spielen beschäftigt).	● Etwas geschieht gerade.

31   I like going for walks

Do you like going to the cinema? I like going for walks. Aber: I'd like to go out tonight. Vgl. 35	Gehen Sie gern ins Kino? Ich gehe gern spazieren.	● Die *ing-form (going, doing)* steht oft nach *like,* um auszudrücken, daß man etwas gern tut.

Zukunft

32   Will

I'll go by train. I think I'll hire a car. He'll be late.	Ich werde mit dem Zug fahren. Ich glaube, ich werde einen Wagen mieten. Er wird zu spät kommen.	● *I'll* (Kurzform von *I will*) drückt die Zukunft aus (ich werde). *Will* kann in allen Personen verwendet werden.
Aber: Shall we go out tonight?	Sollen wir heute abend ausgehen?	● *Shall* steht meist in Fragen mit *we* oder *I.*

33   Going to

I'm going to have a party on Saturday. Tom's going to see a friend at the weekend. They're going to hire a car.	Ich werde am Samstag eine Party geben (= beabsichtige). Tom wird am Wochenende einen Freund besuchen. Sie werden ein Auto mieten.	● Die Zukunft kann auch durch *be (am, is, are) going to* ausgedrückt werden. Es deutet an, daß man etwas *plant, will, beabsichtigt.*

34   I'm coming

I'm coming to London on Tuesday. She's leaving Paris on Monday. He's going on holiday/to Brighton. What are you doing at the weekend?	Ich komme am Dienstag nach London (werde kommen). Sie fährt am Montag von Paris ab (wird abfahren). Er fährt auf Urlaub/nach Brighton. Was machst du am Wochenende?	● Mitunter wird die Zukunft auch durch das *Present Continuous* ausgedrückt. Besonders gilt dies für die Verben *go, come* und *leave,* wenn etwas geplant ist.

35 I'd like to

I'd like to go out tonight.	Ich möchte heute abend (gern) ausgehen.	● Wünsche werden durch *I'd like to* . . . *(I'd = I would)* ausgedrückt. Fragen mit *Would you like to* . . .?
Would you like to go to the cinema?	Würden Sie gern ins Kino gehen?	
When would you like to go?	Wann möchten Sie gehen?	● In der Antwort kann das Verb nach *I'd like to* entfallen.
I'd like to very much.	Ich möchte (es) sehr gern.	

36 Fragewörter

What's that?	Was ist das?
What about a theatre?	Wie wär's mit einem Theater(stück)?
What time are you coming?	Um welche Zeit kommst du?
What time is it?	
What's the time?	Wie spät ist es?
What's he like?	Wie ist er?
Which floor do you live on?	In welchem Stock wohnst du?
Who's that woman?	Wer ist diese Frau?
When are you coming?	Wann kommst du?
Where is he now?	Wo ist er jetzt?
Where are you going?	Wohin gehst du?
Where is she from?	Woher ist/stammt sie?
I'm going on holiday. — Where to?	Ich gehe auf Urlaub. — Wohin?
Why are you late?	Warum hast du dich verspätet?
How old are you?	Wie alt bist du?
How many girls are there?	Wieviele Mädchen gibt es?
How much is it?	Was kostet es?
How big is the table?	Wie groß ist der Tisch?
How far is it to London?	Wie weit ist es bis (nach) London?
How long are you staying?	Wie lange bleibst du?
How often do you see him?	Wie oft siehst du ihn?

Land	Adjektiv, Sprache	Einwohner (Singular/Plural)
America [ə'merɪkə]	American [ə'merɪkən]	an/the American(s) [ə'merɪkən(z)]
Australia [ɒ'streɪljə]	Australian [ɒ'streɪljən]	an/the Australian(s) [ɒ'streɪljən(z)]
(Great) Britain ['brɪtn]	British ['brɪtɪʃ]	a Britisher/the British ['brɪtɪʃ(ə)]
China ['tʃaɪnə]	Chinese [tʃaɪ'niːz]	a/the Chinese [tʃaɪ'niːz]
Denmark ['denmɑːk]	Danish ['deɪnɪʃ]	a/the Dane(s) [deɪn(z)]
England ['ɪŋglənd]	English ['ɪŋglɪʃ]	an Englishman/the English ['ɪŋglɪʃ(mən)]
Europe ['jʊərəp]	European [jʊərə'pɪən]	a/the European(s) [jʊərə'pɪən(z)]
Finland ['fɪnlənd]	Finnish ['fɪnɪʃ]	a/the Finn(s) [fɪn(z)]
France [frɑːns]	French [frentʃ]	a/the French [frentʃ]
Germany ['dʒɜːmənɪ]	German ['dʒɜːmən]	a/the German(s) ['dʒɜːmən(z)]
Greece [griːs]	Greek [griːk]	a/the Greek(s) [griːk(s)]
Holland ['hɒlənd]	Dutch [dʌtʃ]	a Dutchman/the Dutch ['dʌtʃ(mən)]
Ireland ['aɪələnd]	Irish ['aɪərɪʃ]	an Irishman/the Irish ['aɪərɪʃ(mən)]
Italy ['ɪtəlɪ]	Italien [ɪ'tæljən]	an/the Italian(s) [ɪ'tæljən(z)]
Norway ['nɔːweɪ]	Norwegian [nɔː'wiːdʒən]	a/the Norwegian(s) [nɔː'wiːdʒən(z)]
Russia ['rʌʃə]	Russian ['rʌʃən]	a/the Russian(s) ['rʌʃən(z)]
Scotland ['skɒtlənd]	Scottish ['skɒtɪʃ]	a Scot(sman)/the Scots ['skɒts(mən)]
Spain [speɪn]	Spanish ['spænɪʃ]	a Spaniard/the Spanish ['spænjəd, 'spænɪʃ]
Sweden ['swiːdn]	Swedish ['swiːdɪʃ]	a/the Swede(s) [swiːd(z)]
Turkey ['tɜːkɪ]	Turkish ['tɜːkɪʃ]	a/the Turk(s) [tɜːk(s)]
the United States [ðə juː'naɪtɪd 'steɪts]	American [ə'merɪkən]	an/the American(s) [ə'merɪkən(z)]
Wales [weɪlz]	Welsh [welʃ]	a Welshman/the Welsh ['welʃ(mən)]
Yugoslavia [juːgəʊ'slɑːvjə]	Yugoslav(ian) [juːgəʊ'slɑːv(jən)]	a/the Yugoslav(s) [juːgəʊ'slɑːv(z)]

● Alle Nationalitätsbezeichnungen werden mit großem Anfangsbuchstaben geschrieben.

● Die Adjektive bezeichnen auch die Sprache: *English* = das Englische, die englische Sprache.

● Die Personenbezeichnungen auf *-man* haben zwei Pluralformen:
 a) mit *-men* zur Bezeichnung mehrerer Personen *(two Englishmen, two Frenchmen, three Irishmen, two Scotsmen);*
 b) mit *the* zur Bezeichnung der Gesamtheit eines Volkes (*the English* = die, alle Engländer; *the Dutch* = die, alle Holländer; *the Scots* = die, alle Schotten).

● Die anderen bilden den Plural mit *-s: two Americans, three Germans, the Germans, the Swedes.*

38 **Großschreibung**

It is Monday morning.	Es ist Montag vormittag.	● Im Englischen werden groß geschrieben:
Can I help you?	Kann ich Ihnen helfen?	Wochentage;
Excuse me, are you Mr Petersen?	Entschuldigen Sie, sind Sie Herr Petersen?	das Personalpronomen *I;*
The little black bag belongs to Miss Dupont.	Die kleine schwarze Tasche gehört Fräulein Dupont.	*Mr, Mrs, Miss;* Nationalitätsbezeichnungen.
I'm English.	Ich bin Engländer(in).	

Aussprache und Lautschrift

Um die Wörterverzeichnisse in *All Right* und das eigene Wörterbuch voll ausnützen zu können, ist die Beherrschung der Lautschrift, der phonetischen Umschrift, notwendig. Sie beschreibt nicht nur, wie man ein Wort ausspricht, sondern auch, wie man es betont. In der Lautschrift werden z. T. bekannte Buchstaben verwendet, z. B. [e, t, r], z. T. aber auch besondere Zeichen für bestimmte Laute, z. B. [ʃ] für den sch-Laut oder [ʊ] für das kurze u.
Die Lautschrift steht immer in eckigen Klammern [ ].
Das Betonungszeichen ['] bedeutet, daß die folgende Silbe betont wird, z. B. *goodbye* [gʊdˈbaɪ] = die zweite Silbe [-ˈbaɪ] ist betont.

Vokale — Diphthonge — Konsonanten

Man kann die Laute in drei Gruppen einteilen:
Vokale (Selbstlaute), z. B. [e, ɑː, uː];
Diphthonge (Doppellaute), z. B. [aʊ];
Konsonanten (Mitlaute), z. B. [t, d, l].
Der Doppelpunkt [ː] deutet an, daß der Vokal lang ausgesprochen wird, z. B. *eat* [iːt]. Zur deutlichen Unterscheidung werden außerdem für die kurzen Vokale etwas abweichende Zeichen verwendet, z. B. [ɪ] ohne Punkt für das kurze i, z. B. *it* [ɪt].

Lautschrift

Vokale

kurz Beispiel		wie im dt.	lang Beispiel		wie im dt.
[ɪ]	in [ɪn]	in	[iː]	see [siː]	Sie
[ʊ]	put [pʊt]	Mutter	[uː]	school [skuːl]	Schule (etwas offener, mit Lippenrundung)
[ɒ]	box [bɒks]	boxen (kurzes, offenes o)	[ɔː]	door [dɔː]	Tor (langes, offenes o)
[ə]	better [ˈbetə]	bitte (kurzes, unbetontes e)	[ɜː]	first [fɜːst]	fördern (ohne r-Laut und ohne Lippenrundung)
[ʌ]	come [kʌm]	Kamm (kurzes a, etwas geschlossener als dt.)	[ɑː]	father [ˈfɑːðə]	Vater (langes a)
[e]	bed [bed]	Bett (kurzes e)			
[æ]	hat [hæt]	hätte (kurzes offenes ä)			

Diphthonge

Diphthonge sind Doppellaute, bei denen die Stimme von einem Vokal zum anderen hinübergleitet, z. B. [əʊ] vom kurzen [ə] wie in bitt**e** zum kurzen [ʊ] wie in **B**utter gleitend.

[aɪ]	fine [faɪn]	fein	[aʊ]	how [haʊ]	Haus
[ɔɪ]	boy [bɔɪ]	Beute	[əʊ]	no [nəʊ]	von [ə] zu [ʊ] gleitend
[eɪ]	name [neɪm]	von [e] zu [ɪ] gleitend	[eə]	bear [beə]	Bär
[ɪə]	here [hɪə]	hier			

Konsonanten

stimm-haft	Beispiel	wie im dt.	stimm-los	Beispiel	wie im dt.
[z]	easy ['i:zɪ]	sie (stimmhaftes s)	[s]	sun [sʌn]	wissen (stimmloses s)
[ʒ]	television ['telɪvɪʒn]	Garage	[ʃ]	fish [fɪʃ]	Fisch
			[tʃ]	church [tʃɜ:tʃ]	deutsch
[dʒ]	just [dʒʌst]	Dschungel	[θ]	thing [θɪŋ]	stimmloses s „gelispelt", Zunge
[ð]	father ['fɑ:ðə]	stimmhaftes s „gelispelt", Zunge an obere Vorderzähne, weiter vorn im Mund als [z]			an obere Vorderzähne, weiter vorn im Mund als [s]
[r]	red [red]	Zunge vom Gaumen leicht zurückbiegen, nicht rollen, kein Rachen-r			
[ŋ]	long [lɒŋ]	lang (ohne k-Laut)			
[w]	white [waɪt]	[u:] mit vorgestülpten Lippen			
[v]	very ['verɪ]	Ware (Oberzähne auf die Unterlippe)			

Zu beachten:

● Stimmhafte Konsonanten [b, d, g] dürfen im Englischen am Wortende nicht stimmlos zu [p, t, k] werden: hand [hænd], dog [dɒg]. Vgl. dt. Hund [hʊnt], Tag [tɑ:k].

● s am Wortanfang wird im Englischen immer stimmlos [s] gesprochen: sun [sʌn], sit [sɪt]. Vgl. dt. Sonne ['zɒnə], sitzen ['zɪtsən].

Das englische Alphabet

A [eɪ]	D [di:]	G [dʒi:]	J [dʒeɪ]	M [em]	P [pi:]	S [es]	V [vi:]	Y [waɪ]
B [bi:]	E [i:]	H [eɪtʃ]	K [keɪ]	N [en]	Q [kju:]	T [ti:]	W ['dʌblju:]	Z [zed,
C [si:]	F [ef]	I [aɪ]	L [el]	O [əʊ]	R [ɑ:]	U [ju:]	X [eks]	Am. zi:]

Eigennamen des Buches und der Rollenkarten

(the) Albert Hall
 [ðɪ ˈælbət ˈhɔːl]
Antonio's [ænˈtəʊnɪəʊz]
George Appleby
 [dʒɔːdʒ ˈæplbɪ]
Pete Armour [piːt ˈɑːmə]
Gloria Ashley [ˈglɔːrɪə ˈæʃlɪ]
Jean Atkins [dʒiːn ˈætkɪnz]
John Austin [dʒɒn ˈɒstɪn]
Bach [bɑːx]
Baker Street [ˈbeɪkə striːt]
Joan Baker [dʒəʊn ˈbeɪkə]
Baltimore [ˈbɔːltɪmɔː]
Duncan Bates [ˈdʌŋkən ˈbeɪts]
Bath [bɑːθ]
June Baxter [dʒuːn ˈbækstə]
Bayswater [ˈbeɪzwɔːtə]
Maria Berg [məˈrɪə bɜːg]
Berlin [bɜːˈlɪn]
Monica Best [ˈmɒnɪkə ˈbest]
Birmingham [ˈbɜːmɪŋəm]
Sheila Black [ˈʃiːlə ˈblæk]
George Blake [dʒɔːdʒ ˈbleɪk]
Bradford [ˈbrædfəd]
Glenda Brian [ˈglendə ˈbraɪən]
Charles Briggs [tʃɑːlz brɪgz]
Brighton [ˈbraɪtn]
Tony Brown [ˈtəʊnɪ ˈbraʊn]
Bruce [bruːs]
Alison Burke [ˈælɪsn ˈbɜːk]
Linda Burns [ˈlɪndə ˈbɜːnz]
Judith Burton [ˈdʒuːdɪθ ˈbɜːtn]
Cambridge [ˈkeɪmbrɪdʒ]
Canberra [ˈkænbərə]
Peter Carr [ˈpiːtə ˈkɑː]
Barbara Carter
 [ˈbɑːbərə ˈkɑːtə]
Chancery Lane
 [ˈtʃɑːnsərɪ ˈleɪn]
Chinatown [ˈtʃaɪnətaʊn]
Chung Ho [tʃʌŋ ˈhəʊ]
Alan Clark [ˈælən ˈklɑːk]
Tina Close [ˈtiːnə ˈkləʊs]
Cologne [kəˈləʊn] Köln
Copenhagen [kəʊpnˈheɪgən]

Cornwall [ˈkɔːnwəl]
Harold Cripps [ˈhærəld ˈkrɪps]
Edward Cross [ˈedwəd ˈkrɒs]
David Crown [ˈdeɪvɪd ˈkraʊn]
Ann Dixon [æn ˈdɪksn]
Betty Dobson [ˈbetɪ ˈdɒbsn]
Doncaster [ˈdɒŋkəstə]
Tom Driver [tɒm ˈdraɪvə]
Dupont [ˈdjuːpɒnt]
Edinburgh [ˈedɪnbərə]
Marion Ellis [ˈmeərɪən ˈelɪs]
Embankment [ɪmˈbæŋkmənt]
Euston [ˈjuːstən]
Falls [fɔːlz]
Allan Ford [ˈælən ˈfɔːd]
Jean Fox [dʒiːn fɒks]
Stephen Frick [ˈstiːvn ˈfrɪk]
Clark Gable [klɑːk ˈgeɪbl]
Bill Gardiner [bɪl ˈgɑːdnə]
George IV [ˈdʒɔːdʒ ðə ˈfɔːθ]
James Gibson [dʒeɪmz ˈgɪbsn]
Eric Goodman [ˈerɪk ˈgʊdmən]
Greenbaum [ˈgriːnbaʊm]
Joe Hackett [dʒəʊ ˈhækɪt]
Brian Hammond
 [ˈbraɪən ˈhæmənd]
Hanover [ˈhænəʊvə]
 Hannover
Patrick Harrison
 [ˈpætrɪk ˈhærɪsn]
Harrogate [ˈhærəʊgɪt]
Hastings [ˈheɪstɪŋz]
Ann Hill [æn hɪl]
Albert Hobbs [ˈælbət ˈhɒbz]
Holborn [ˈhəʊbən]
Monica Horn [ˈmɒnɪkə ˈhɔːn]
Leslie Howard [ˈlezlɪ ˈhaʊəd]
Mary Hudson [ˈmeərɪ ˈhʌdsn]
(the) Isle of Wight
 [ðɪ ˈaɪl əv ˈwaɪt]
Alan Jackson [ˈælən ˈdʒæksn]
Jaguar [ˈdʒægjʊə]
Elsie James [ˈelsɪ ˈdʒeɪmz]
Sandra Johnson
 [ˈsændrə ˈdʒɒnsn]

Robert Columbus Jones
 [ˈrɒbət kəˈlʌmbəs ˈdʒəʊnz]
John Kidd [dʒɒn kɪd]
Anne Kling [æn klɪŋ]
Lady Jane's [ˈleɪdɪ ˈdʒeɪnz]
Land's End [lændz ˈend]
Pat Lane [pæt leɪn]
Barbara Lang [ˈbɑːbərə ˈlæŋ]
Leeds [liːdz]
Leicester Square
 [ˈlestə ˈskweə]
Vivien Leigh [ˈvɪvɪən ˈliː]
Lisbon [ˈlɪzbən]
 Lissabon
Littlehampton [ˈlɪtlhæmptən]
Penny Lockwood
 [ˈpenɪ ˈlɒkwʊd]
London [ˈlʌndən]
Peter Lord [ˈpiːtə ˈlɔːd]
Los Angeles [lɒsˈændʒɪliːz]
(the) Lyric [ðə ˈlɪrɪk]
Manchester [ˈmæntʃɪstə]
Marble Arch [ˈmɑːbl ˈɑːtʃ]
Marco [ˈmɑːkəʊ]
Alfred Marks [ˈælfrɪd ˈmɑːks]
George Mikes [dʒɔːdʒ ˈmiːkeʃ]
Ann Mitchell [æn ˈmɪtʃl]
Lynne Moore [lɪn mʊə]
Ethel Morris [ˈeθl ˈmɒrɪs]
Robert Mortimer
 [ˈrɒbət ˈmɔːtɪmə]
Mozart [ˈməʊtsɑːt]
Munich [ˈmjuːnɪk] München
Nanking [nænˈkɪŋ]
Naples [ˈneɪplz] Neapel
Dean Newman [diːn ˈnjuːmən]
New York [njuːˈjɔːk]
Nuremberg [ˈnjʊərəmbɜːg]
 Nürnberg
Penny Oakes [ˈpenɪ ˈəʊks]
(the) Odeon [ðɪ ˈəʊdjən]
Oslo [ˈɒzləʊ]
Oxford (Circus)
 [ˈɒksfəd (ˈsɜːkəs)]
(the) Palladium [pəˈleɪdjəm]

Paris ['pærɪs]
Pat Parker [pæt 'pɑːkə]
Rosemary Peters
['rəʊzmərɪ 'piːtəz]
Alex, Margret Petersen
['ælɪks, 'mɑːgrɪt 'piːtəsn]
Jennifer Plowman
['dʒenɪfə 'plaʊmən]
Peter Potter ['piːtə 'pɒtə]
Queensway ['kwiːnzweɪ]
Joan Randall [dʒəʊn 'rændl]
Susan Reynolds
['suːzn 'renldz]
Sally Richardson
['sælɪ 'rɪtʃədsn]
Martha Roberts
['mɑːθə 'rɒbəts]
Albert Robins ['ælbət 'rɒbɪnz]
Fred Robinson [fred 'rɒbɪnsn]
George Rolls [dʒɔːdʒ rəʊlz]
Rolls-Royce [rəʊlz'rɔɪs]
Martin Rose ['mɑːtɪn 'rəʊz]
(the) Royal Pavilion
[ðə 'rɔɪəl pə'vɪljən]
Johnny Sands ['dʒɒnɪ 'sændz]

San Francisco
[sænfrən'sɪskəʊ]
Shakespeare ['ʃeɪkspɪə]
Louise Short [luːˈiːz 'ʃɔːt]
Elisabeth Silver
[ɪ'lɪzəbəθ 'sɪlvə]
Jim Silverberg
[dʒɪm 'sɪlvəbɜːg]
Monique Simon
[mə'niːk 'saɪmən]
Robin Slater ['rɒbɪn 'sleɪtə]
Jack Smith [dʒæk smɪθ]
Soho ['səʊhəʊ]
South Pacific ['saʊθ pə'sɪfɪk]
Bob Spence [bɒb spens]
Eric Spencer ['erɪk 'spensə]
Susan Steadman
['suːzn 'stedmən]
Rita Stern ['riːtə 'stɜːn]
Mark Stevens [mɑːk 'stiːvnz]
Stockholm ['stɒkhəʊm]
Stoke [stəʊk]
Karen Stone ['kɑːrən 'stəʊn]
Stratford ['strætfəd]
Sussex ['sʌsɪks]

Swansea ['swɒnzɪ]
Sydney ['sɪdnɪ]
Helen Tanner ['helɪn 'tænə]
Irene Thompson
['aɪriːn 'tɒmpsn]
Jean Todd [dʒiːn tɒd]
Tokyo ['təʊkjəʊ] Tokio
Tottenham Court Road
['tɒtnəm kɔːt 'rəʊd]
Trafalgar Square
[trə'fælgə 'skweə]
Travers ['trævəz]
Julie Trent ['dʒuːlɪ 'trent]
Tring [trɪŋ]
Waterloo [wɔːtə'luː]
Wembley ['wemblɪ]
Tom Wendel [tɒm 'wendl]
Carol White ['kærəl 'waɪt]
Jenny Wilson ['dʒenɪ 'wɪlsn]
Peter Winter ['piːtə 'wɪntə]
Barbara Wolf ['bɑːbərə 'wʊlf]
Bob Word [bɒb wɜːd]
York [jɔːk]
Frank Zappa [fræŋk 'zæpə]

Wörterverzeichnis

1. Sorry I'm late

(I'm) sorry [aım 'spri]	Verzeihung, (es) tut mir leid
late [leıt]	spät
I'm late	ich habe mich verspätet
Sorry, I'm late	Es tut mir leid, daß ich mich verspätet habe
it is [ıt 'ız]	es ist
at [æt]	an, auf
London ['lʌndən]	London
airport ['eəpɔ:t]	Flughafen
Monday ['mʌndı]	Montag
morning ['mɔ:nıŋ]	Morgen, Vormittag
Oh, my God ['əʊ maı 'gɒd]	Oh, Gott; Ach du meine Güte
after ['ɑ:ftə]	nach
ten [ten]	zehn
excuse me [ık'skju:z mı]	entschuldigen Sie, Verzeihung
are you [ɑ: 'ju:]	sind Sie, bist du
Mr (= Mister) ['mıstə]	Herr (vor Namen)
No, I'm not [nəʊ aım 'nɒt]	Nein, ich bin es nicht
Oh, sorry.	Oh, entschuldigen Sie.
Yes, that's right. ['jes ðæts 'raıt]	Ja, das stimmt.
That's all right.	Das macht (doch) nichts.
from [frɒm]	von
Universal Services [ju:nı'vɜ:sl 'sɜ:vısız]	Name einer Firma für allgemeine Dienstleistungen
the [ðə, vor Vokalen ðı]	der, die, das
office ['ɒfıs]	Büro
this [ðıs]	dies(er, e, es); das
my [maı]	mein(e)
wife [waıf]	(Ehe-)Frau
Hullo [hə'ləʊ]	Hallo, Guten Tag (usw.)
here's [hıəz] = **here is** [hıər'ız]	hier ist
a/an [ə(n)]	ein(e)
brochure ['brəʊʃə]	Broschüre, Prospekt
What's on ['wɒts 'ɒn]	Was ist los, gibt es
in [ın]	in
Thank you. [θæŋk jʊ]	Danke.

and [ænd]	und
card [kɑ:d]	Karte
that [ðæt]	das (da)
girl friend ['gɜ:l frend]	Freundin
photo ['fəʊtəʊ]	Photo(graphie)
shall [ʃæl]	sollen
we [wı]	wir
go [gəʊ]	gehen
then [ðen]	dann
Shall we go, then?	Wollen wir dann gehen?
All right.	In Ordnung. Okay.
your [jɔ:]	dein(e); Ihr(e)
problem ['prɒbləm]	Problem
our ['aʊə]	unser(e)
assistant manager [ə'sıstənt 'mænıdʒə]	Chefassistent
Tel. = telephone ['telıfəʊn]	Telefon
better ['betə]	besser
than [ðæn]	als
never ['nevə]	nie(mals)

How to say it

how [haʊ]	wie
to [tʊ]	zu
say [seı]	sagen
How to say it	Wie man etwas sagt
meet [mi:t]	(jdn) treffen
introduce [ıntrə'dju:s]	vorstellen
people ['pi:pl]	Leute
meeting and introducing people	jdn treffen und vorstellen
Are you? [ɑ: jʊ]	Sind Sie (es wirklich)?
secretary ['sekrətrı]	Sekretär(in)
engineer [endʒı'nıə]	Ingenieur
German ['dʒɜ:mən]	deutsch
English ['ıŋglıʃ]	englisch
now [naʊ]	nun, jetzt
make [meık]	machen, bilden
sentence ['sentəns]	Satz
like this [laık 'ðıs]	so, in dieser Art
about [ə'baʊt]	über
yourself [jɔ:'self]	sich, dich selbst

Now make sentences like this about yourself.

work [wɜ:k] — arbeiten

pair [peə] — Paar

Work in pairs. — Arbeiten Sie mit einem Partner.

Mrs ['mɪsɪz] — Frau (vor Namen)

Miss [mɪs] — Fräulein (meist vor Namen)

nurse [nɜ:s] — Krankenschwester, -pfleger(in)

Swedish ['swi:dɪʃ] — schwedisch

American [ə'merɪkən] — amerikanisch

Are you American? — Sind Sie Amerikaner?

question ['kwestʃən] — Frage

husband ['hʌzbənd] — (Ehe-)Mann

phrase [freɪz] — Wendung, Ausdruck

practise ['præktɪs] — üben

these [ði:z] — diese (hier)

Practise saying these phrases. — Üben Sie, diese Wendungen zu sprechen.

see [si:] — sehen

exercise ['eksəsaɪz] — Übung

Exercise 1

one [wʌn] — eins

put [pʊt] — setzen, stellen, legen

together [tə'geðə] — zusammen

with [wɪð] — mit

right [raɪt] — richtig

Put the sentences in A together with the right sentences in B. — Ordnen Sie die Sätze in A den richtigen Sätzen in B zu.

pilot ['paɪlət] — Pilot

Exercise 2

two [tu:] — zwei

write [raɪt] — schreiben

answer ['ɑ:nsə] — Antwort

under ['ʌndə] — unter

picture ['pɪktʃə] — Bild

Write the questions and answers under the pictures. — Schreiben Sie die Fragen und Antworten unter die Bilder.

woman ['wʊmən] — Frau

man [mæn] — Mann

boy [bɔɪ] — Junge

girl [gɜ:l] — Mädchen

Exercise 3

three [θri:] — drei

someone ['sʌmwʌn] — jemand(en)

introducing someone — jemanden vorstellen

one [wʌn] — ein(e)

person ['pɜ:sn] — Person

another [ə'nʌðə] — ein(e) andere(r, s)

In the picture one person is introducing another person. — Auf dem Bild stellt eine Person jemand anderen vor.

mother ['mʌðə] — Mutter

father ['fɑ:ðə] — Vater

Exercise 4

four [fɔ:] — vier

role play ['rəʊl pleɪ] — Rollenspiel

teacher ['ti:tʃə] — Lehrer(in), Kursleiter(in)

will [wɪl] — werden, wird

give [gɪv] — geben

you [ju:] — Ihnen; dir

more [mɔ:] — mehr

information [ɪnfə'meɪʃn] — Information(en)

Your teacher will give you more information. — Ihr Kursleiter wird Ihnen weitere Informationen geben.

Exercise 5

five [faɪv] — fünf

landing card ['lændɪŋ kɑ:d] — Einreisekarte

fill in [fɪl 'ɪn] — ausfüllen, einsetzen

The Petersens fill in landing cards at London Airport. — Die Petersens füllen auf dem Londoner Flughafen Einreisekarten aus.

immigration act [ɪmɪ'greɪʃn ækt] — Einwanderungsgesetz

family name ['fæmɪlɪ neɪm] — Familienname

block letters ['blɒk letəz] — Druckbuchstaben, Versalien

forename ['fɔ:neɪm] — Vorname

occupation [ɒkjʊ'peɪʃn] — Beruf

design engineer [dɪ'zaɪn endʒɪ'nɪə] — Ingenieur für Formgebung

date of birth ['deɪt əv 'bɜ:θ] — Geburtsdatum

place of birth ['pleɪs əv 'bɜ:θ] — Geburtsort

sex [seks] — Geschlecht

male [meɪl]	männlich
nationality [næʃəˈnæləti]	Nationalität, Staatsange-
	hörigkeit
signature [ˈsɪgnətʃə]	Unterschrift
full [fʊl]	voll(ständig)
address [əˈdres]	Adresse, Anschrift
United Kingdom [juːˈnaɪtɪd ˈkɪŋdəm]	Vereinigtes Königreich (England, Schottland, Wales, Nordirland)
centre [ˈsentə]	Zentrum
hotel [həʊˈtel]	Hotel
for official use [fər əˈfɪʃl ˈjuːs]	für amtliche Vermerke

Exercise 6

six [sɪks]	sechs
job [dʒɒb]	Beruf
Write the questions and answers about these people's jobs.	Schreiben Sie die Fragen und Antworten zu den Berufen dieser Leute.
for example [fər ɪgˈzɑːmpl]	zum Beispiel
use [juːz]	benutzen, gebrauchen, verwenden
word [wɜːd]	Wort
Use these words.	Benutze diese Wörter.
typist [ˈtaɪpɪst]	Maschinenschreiber(in), Typistin
bus driver [ˈbʌs draɪvə]	Busfahrer(in)
housewife [ˈhaʊswaɪf]	Hausfrau
shop assistant [ˈʃɒp əˈsɪstənt]	Verkäufer(in)
policeman [pəˈliːsmən]	Polizist
business man [ˈbɪznɪsmən]	Geschäftsmann
waiter [ˈweɪtə]	Kellner
taxi driver [ˈtæksɪ draɪvə]	Taxifahrer
cook [kʊk]	Koch, Köchin
bank clerk [ˈbæŋk klɑːk]	Bankangestellte(r)
student [ˈstjuːdnt]	Student(in)
traffic warden [ˈtræfɪk wɔːdn]	Verkehrswächter

Exercise 7

seven [ˈsevn]	sieben
British [ˈbrɪtɪʃ]	britisch
passport [ˈpɑːspɔːt]	Paß

Exercise 8

eight [eɪt]	acht
translate [trænsˈleɪt]	übersetzen
into [ˈɪntʊ]	in (hinein)

Translate these sentences into German.	Übersetzen Sie diese Sätze ins Deutsche.
idiomatic [ɪdɪəˈmætɪk]	idiomatisch, dem Sprachgebrauch entsprechend
Use idiomatic German.	Verwenden Sie idiomatisches Deutsch.
try [traɪ]	versuchen
look at [lʊk ət]	ansehen
above [əˈbʌv]	oben
Try not to look at the sentences above.	Versuchen Sie, nicht die obigen Sätze anzusehen.

Exercise 9

nine [naɪn]	neun
who [huː]	wer
has [hæz]	hat
what [wɒt]	welche(r, s, n)
Who has what job?	Wer hat welchen Beruf?
read [riːd]	lesen
Read the information about the people.	Lesen Sie die Informationen über die Leute.
then [ðen]	dann
so that [səʊ ðət]	so daß
can [kæn]	können, kann(st), könnt
say [seɪ]	sagen
Then put the information together, so that you can say who has what job.	Fügen Sie dann die Informationen zusammen, so daß Sie sagen können, wer welchen Beruf hat.
he [hiː]	er
she [ʃiː]	sie
film star [ˈfɪlm stɑː]	Filmstar
surname [ˈsɜːneɪm]	Nach-, Familienname

London Airport, Heathrow

foreign [ˈfɒrɪn]	ausländisch, fremd
Commonwealth [ˈkɒmənwelθ]	Staatenbund Großbritanniens mit ehemaligen Kolonien
Irish Republic [ˈaɪərɪʃ rɪˈpʌblɪk]	Irische Republik
if [ɪf]	wenn, falls
can't [kɑːnt] = cannot [ˈkænɒt]	nicht können
answer [ˈɑːnsə]	(be-)antworten
them [ðem]	sie, ihnen
again [əˈgen]	wieder, noch einmal
If you can't answer them,	Wenn Sie sie nicht beant-

read the text and then try again. — worten können, lesen Sie den Text und versuchen Sie es dann noch einmal.

passenger ['pæsɪndʒə] — Passagier, (Fahr-, Flug-)Gast·

terminal ['tɜːmɪnl] — Abfertigungshalle (im Flughafen)

(air) terminal — Haltestelle, Stadtbüro für Zubringerbus zum Flughafen

flight [flaɪt] — Flug
to Europe [tʊ 'jʊərəp] — nach Europa
do [duː] — tun, machen
BA = British Airways [biːˈeɪ, 'brɪtɪʃ 'eəweɪz] —
go [gəʊ] — gehen
LH = Lufthansa —
must [mʌst] — müssen, muß(t), müßt
check in [tʃek 'ɪn] — sich abfertigen lassen
minute ['mɪnɪt] — Minute
before [bɪˈfɔː] — (be-)vor
their [ðeə] — ihr(e)
departure [dɪˈpɑːtʃə] — Abflug, Abfahrt
coach [kəʊtʃ] — (Flughafen-, Reise-)Bus
leave [liːv] — verlassen
bring [brɪŋ] — (mit-)bringen
into ['ɪntʊ] — in (hinein)
bring into — einführen
Britain ['brɪtn] — (Groß-)Britannien
100 = a, one hundred ['hʌndrəd] — hundert
cigarette [sɪgəˈret] — Zigarette
bottle ['bɒtl] — Flasche
whisky ['wɪskɪ] — Whisky
wine [waɪn] — Wein
travel with ['trævl 'wɪð] — reisen, fliegen, fahren mit
all [ɔːl] — alle
other ['ʌðə] — andere(r, s, n)
airline ['eəlaɪn] — Fluglinie, -gesellschaft
e.g. = for example [fər ɪgˈzɑːmpl] — z. B., zum Beispiel
SAS = Scandinavian Airlines System ['es eɪ 'es skændɪˈneɪvjən 'eəlaɪnz 'sɪstəm] —
KLM ['keɪ el 'em] — Royal Dutch Airlines
etc. = and so on [ənd səʊ 'ɒn] — usw., und so weiter

right [raɪt] — richtig
there [ðeə] — dort, da
there are [ðeə 'rɑː, 'ðərə] — es gibt
tax-free ['tæks friː] — zollfrei
shop [ʃɒp] — Laden, Geschäft
both [bəʊθ] — beide
allowance [əˈlaʊəns] — erlaubte Menge
or [ɔː] — oder
ounce [aʊns] — Unze (= 28 Gramm)
gram [græm] — Gramm
tobacco [təˈbækəʊ] — Tabak
litre ['liːtə] — Liter
spirits ['spɪrɪts] — Spirituosen, Alkohol

Opinions

opinion [əˈpɪnjən] — Meinung, Ansicht
why [waɪ] — warum
study ['stʌdɪ] — studieren, lernen
Why are you studying English? — Warum lernen Sie Englisch?
need [niːd] — brauchen
for [fə] — für
work [wɜːk] — Arbeit
think [θɪŋk] — denken, glauben
it's fun [fʌn] — es macht Spaß
want [wɒnt] — wollen
England ['ɪŋglənd] — England

2. How are you?

How are you? — Wie geht es (Ihnen)?
take to [teɪk] — bringen zu (in, nach)
evening ['iːvnɪŋ] — Abend
reception [rɪˈsepʃn] — Empfang
fine [faɪn] — schön
Fine, thanks. [θæŋks] — Danke, gut.
All right, thanks. — Danke, gut.
cold [kəʊld] — kalt
today [təˈdeɪ] — heute
Cold today, isn't it? — (Es ist) Kalt heute, nicht wahr?
horrible ['hɒrəbl] — furchtbar, schrecklich
good [gʊd] — gut
form [fɔːm] — Formular
please [pliːz] — bitte
Will you fill in this form, please. — Würden Sie bitte dieses Formular ausfüllen?
room [ruːm] — Zimmer

number ['nʌmbə]	Nummer, Zahl
well [wel]	nun
mean [mi:n]	meinen
Penny, you mean?	Meinst du Penny?
Wednesday ['wenzdɪ]	Mittwoch
See you on Wednesday.	Wir sehen uns am Mittwoch.
at the pub [pʌb]	im Pub
Cheerio. [tʃɪərɪ'əʊ]	Tschüs.
Goodbye. [gʊd'baɪ]	Auf Wiedersehn.
for all your help [help]	für all Ihre Hilfe

How to say it

greeting ['gri:tɪŋ]	Begrüßung
ask for ['ɑ:sk fə]	bitten um
asking for and giving information	Informationen erfragen und geben
What's your name, please?	Wie heißen Sie bitte?
forget [fə'get]	vergessen
Don't forget to say please.	Vergessen Sie nicht, „bitte" zu sagen.
married ['mærɪd]	verheiratet
doctor ['dɒktə]	Doktor, Arzt
Isn't he?	(Ist er es) Wirklich nicht?
nice and warm [wɔ:m]	schön warm
wet [wet]	naß, regnerisch
windy ['wɪndɪ]	windig
eleven [ɪ'levn]	elf
twelve [twelv]	zwölf
day [deɪ]	Tag
Sunday ['sʌndɪ]	Sonntag
Tuesday ['tju:zdɪ]	Dienstag
Thursday ['θɜ:zdɪ]	Donnerstag
Friday ['fraɪdɪ]	Freitag
Saturday ['sætədɪ]	Sonnabend, Samstag
afternoon [ɑ:ftə'nu:n]	Nachmittag

Exercise 2

weather ['weðə]	Wetter
conversation [kɒnvə'seɪʃn]	Unterhaltung
lovely ['lʌvlɪ]	wunderschön, reizend
sunny ['sʌnɪ]	sonnig
wonderful ['wʌndəfʊl]	wunderbar, herrlich
beautiful ['bju:təfʊl]	schön
cloudy ['klaʊdɪ]	wolkig, bewölkt
awful ['ɔ:fʊl]	furchtbar, schrecklich
nasty ['nɑ:stɪ]	unangenehm, widerlich

Exercise 3

new [nju:]	neu
bus stop ['bʌs stɒp]	Bushaltestelle

Exercise 4

boyfriend ['bɔɪfrend]	Freund

Exercise 6

below [bɪ'ləʊ]	unten(stehend)
match [mætʃ]	(Fußball-)Spiel
restaurant ['restərɒnt]	Restaurant
station ['steɪʃn]	Bahnhof
party ['pɑ:tɪ]	Party, Gesellschaft

Exercise 7

friend [frend]	Freund(in)

Exercise 8

in the street [stri:t]	auf der Straße
have [hæv]	haben
have a conversation	eine Unterhaltung führen
arrange [ə'reɪndʒ]	verabreden

Exercise 9

at the bank [bæŋk]	auf der Bank
post office ['pəʊst ɒfɪs]	Post(amt)
The Swan [swɒn]	Der Schwan (Name eines Pub)

Exercise 10

hot [hɒt]	heiß
on the left [ɒn ðə 'left]	links, auf der linken Seite

Exercise 11

Who's who?	Wer ist wer?

My pub

over ['əʊvə]	über
thousand ['θaʊznd]	tausend
one of them	einer von ihnen
some [sʌm]	einige
very ['verɪ]	sehr
famous ['feɪməs]	berühmt
like [laɪk]	wie
dirty ['dɜ:tɪ]	schmutzig

lots of [lɒts əv]	viele, eine Menge
tourist [ˈtʊərɪst]	Tourist
go there	gehen dorthin
but [bʌt]	aber
most of them [məʊst]	die meisten von ihnen
just [dʒʌst]	nur
ordinary [ˈɔːdnrɪ]	gewöhnlich
place [pleɪs]	Ort
where [weə]	wo(hin)
for a drink [drɪŋk]	um etwas zu trinken
open [ˈəʊpən]	öffnen
at 10.30 [ten ˈθɜːtɪ]	um halb elf
in the morning / afternoon / evening	morgens, vormittags / nachmittags / abends, am Morgen, Vormittag / Nachmittag / Abend
close [kləʊz]	schließen
for the day	für den Tag
funny [ˈfʌnɪ]	seltsam, komisch
opening times [taɪmz]	Öffnungszeiten
hard [hɑːd]	hart, schwer
interesting [ˈɪntrɪstɪŋ]	interessant
Cheers! [tʃɪəz]	Prost!
landlord [ˈlænlɔːd]	(Gast-)Wirt
wrong [rɒŋ]	falsch
put after	schreiben hinter
is called [kɔːld]	wird genannt, heißt
his [hɪz]	sein(e)
The Rose and Crown [rəʊz, kraʊn]	Rose und Krone

Opinions

favourite [ˈfeɪvərɪt]	Lieblings-
I like beer best.	Ich trinke am liebsten Bier.
footballer [ˈfʊtbɔːlə]	Fußballer
milk [mɪlk]	Milch
a cup of coffee [kʌp əv ˈkɒfɪ]	eine Tasse Kaffee

3. Shall we go out tonight?

shall we [ˈʃæl wɪ]	sollen, wollen wir
go out [gəʊ ˈaʊt]	ausgehen
tonight [təˈnaɪt]	heute abend, nacht
idea [aɪˈdɪə]	Idee
that [ðæt]	jene(r, s)
Would you like . . .? [wʊd]	Möchtest du, würdest du gern . . .?

lady [ˈleɪdɪ]	Dame
strip club [ˈstrɪp klʌb]	Nachtklub mit Striptease
town [taʊn]	Stadt
so [səʊ]	so
No! I don't think so.	Nein, ich glaube nicht.
What about . . .?	Wie wäre es mit . . .?
theatre [ˈθɪətə]	Theater
I'd like [aɪd ˈlaɪk]	ich möchte, würde gern
comedy [ˈkɒmɪdɪ]	Komödie, Lustspiel
who [huː]	der, die das; welche(r, s)
could [kʊd]	konnte
do [duː]	tun, machen
everything [ˈevrɪθɪŋ]	alles
night [naɪt]	Nacht, Abend

How to say it

suggestion [səˈdʒestʃən]	Vorschlag
making suggestions	Vorschläge machen
night club [ˈnaɪt klʌb]	Nachtklub
concert [ˈkɒnsət]	Konzert
dinner [ˈdɪnə]	Abendessen
have dinner	zu Abend essen
cinema [ˈsɪnəmə]	Kino
stay [steɪ]	bleiben
at home [ət ˈhəʊm]	zu Hause
musical [ˈmjuːzɪkl]	Musical
jazz [dʒæz]	Jazz
page [peɪdʒ]	Seite

Exercise 2

he says [sez]	er sagt
pop concert [ˈpɒp ˈkɒnsət]	Schlagerkonzert
watch [wɒtʃ]	beobachten, ansehen
television [ˈtelɪvɪʒn]	Fernsehen; Fernseher
watch television	fernsehen

Exercise 3

missing [ˈmɪsɪŋ]	fehlend
interested [ˈɪntrɪstɪd]	interessiert
end [end]	Ende
in the end	am Ende, schließlich
dialogue [ˈdaɪəlɒg]	Dialog, (Zwie-)Gespräch
let's [lets] = **let us** [ˈlet ʌs] **go**	laß uns gehen, gehen wir

Exercise 5

plan [plæn]	Plan
suggest [səˈdʒest]	vorschlagen

thing [θɪŋ]	Ding, Sache
too [tu:]	auch
serious ['sɪərɪəs]	ernst(haft)
the play [pleɪ]	das Stück
old [əʊld]	alt
music ['mju:zɪk]	Musik
first-class ['fɜ:st klɑ:s]	erstklassig
family ['fæmɪlɪ]	Familie
entertainment [entə'teɪnmənt]	Unterhaltung
symphony ['sɪmfənɪ]	Sinfonie
orchestra ['ɔ:kɪstrə]	Orchester
band wagon ['bænd wægən]	Wagen mit Musikkapelle
rock'n'roll ['rɒkn'rəʊl]	Rock and Roll
noisy ['nɔɪzɪ]	laut, lärmend
expensive [ɪk'spensɪv]	teuer
traditional [trə'dɪʃənl]	traditionell, herkömmlich
food [fu:d]	Nahrung, Essen, Speisen
friendly ['frendlɪ]	freundlich
atmosphere ['ætməsfɪə]	Atmosphäre
real [rɪəl]	wirklich
typical ['tɪpɪkl]	typisch
reasonable ['ri:znəbl]	vernünftig, angemessen
price [praɪs]	Preis
downstairs [daʊn'steəz]	(die Treppe) hinunter, unten
p.m. [pi:'em]	nachmittags
a.am. [eɪ'em]	vormittags
small [smɔ:l]	klein
floor show ['flɔ: ʃəʊ]	Nachtklubvorstellung
disco ['dɪskəʊ]	Disco, Diskothek
young [jʌŋ]	jung
studio ['stju:dɪəʊ]	Studio
Gone with the Wind ['gɒn wɪð ðə 'wɪnd]	Vom Winde verweht
if you have(n't) seen it [hæv(nt)]	wenn Sie es (nicht) gesehen haben
academy [ə'kædəmɪ]	Akademie
trouble ['trʌbl]	Schwierigkeit(en), Sorge(n), Verdruß

Exercise 6

short [ʃɔ:t]	kurz
think of	halten von
ask [ɑ:sk]	fragen
book [bʊk]	Buch
bad [bæd]	schlecht
difficult ['dɪfɪkəlt]	schwer, schwierig
easy ['i:zɪ]	leicht

Exercise 7

crossword (puzzle) ['krɒswɜ:d ('pʌzl)]	Kreuzworträtsel
find [faɪnd]	finden
hidden ['hɪdn]	versteckt, verborgen
there's a good film on at the cinema	im Kino gibt es einen guten Film, läuft ein guter Film

Marco — an Italian waiter

really ['rɪəlɪ]	wirklich, tatsächlich
any ['enɪ]	irgendein(e)
there isn't any work	es gibt keine Arbeit
I came [keɪm]	ich kam
I got [gɒt]	ich bekam
a job as a waiter	eine Anstellung als Kellner
brother ['brʌðə]	Bruder
the pay [peɪ]	Bezahlung, Verdienst
hour ['aʊə]	Stunde
the hours ['aʊəz]	Arbeitszeit
long [lɒŋ]	lang
still [stɪl]	doch
it's got = it has got	es hat
most nights	an den meisten Abenden
we're full [wɪə 'fʊl]	wir sind voll (besetzt)
guess [ges]	glauben
that [ðət]	daß
a lot of [ə 'lɒt əv]	viel(e), eine Menge
money ['mʌnɪ]	Geld
makes a lot of money	verdient viel Geld
had [hæd]	hatte
popular ['pɒpjʊlə]	beliebt

Opinions

tomorrow [tə'mɒrəʊ]	morgen
tomorrow evening	morgen abend

4. A phone call for John

phone [fəʊn]	Telefon
call [kɔ:l]	Anruf, Gespräch
ring [rɪŋ]	klingeln, läuten
flat [flæt]	Wohnung
It's me. [mi:]	Ich bin es.
know [nəʊ]	wissen, kennen

You know.		Du weißt (schon).
of course [əv ˈkɔːs]		natürlich
listen [ˈlɪsn]		(zu-)hören
Listen.		Hör mal.
come [kʌm]		kommen
I'm coming		Ich komme, werde kommen
What time? [taɪm]		Um welche Zeit?
AF = Air France [eɪ ˈef, eə ˈfrɑːns]		
lunch [lʌntʃ]		Mittagessen
have lunch		zu Mittag essen
its [ɪts]		sein(e)
Bye(-bye). [baɪ(ˈbaɪ)]		(Auf) Wiedersehn.
life [laɪf]		(das) Leben
complicated [ˈkɒmplɪkeɪtɪd]		kompliziert

How to say it

at 11 o'clock [əˈklɒk]	um 11 (Uhr)
ticket [ˈtɪkɪt]	(Flug-, Eintritts-)Karte
her [hɜː]	ihr(e)
wallet [ˈwɒlɪt]	Brieftasche
over there [ˈəʊvə ˈðeə]	dort, da drüben
What's the time?	Wie spät ist es?
ask the time [ɑːsk]	nach der Zeit fragen
go home [həʊm]	nach Hause gehen
thirteen [θɜːˈtiːn]	13
fourteen [fɔːˈtiːn]	14
fifteen [fɪfˈtiːn]	15
sixteen [sɪksˈtiːn]	16
seventeen [sevnˈtiːn]	17
eighteen [eɪˈtiːn]	18
nineteen [naɪnˈtiːn]	19
twenty [ˈtwentɪ]	20
thirty [ˈθɜːtɪ]	30
forty [ˈfɔːtɪ]	40
fifty [ˈfɪftɪ]	50

Exercise 2

be [biː]	sein
bus station [ˈbʌs steɪʃn]	Busbahnhof

Exercise 4

diary [ˈdaɪərɪ]	Tagebuch, Kalender
week [wiːk]	Woche

Exercise 5

write out [raɪt ˈaʊt]	ausschreiben

Exercise 6

another [əˈnʌðə]	ein(e) andere(r, s)
country [ˈkʌntrɪ]	Land
phone [fəʊn]	anrufen
to tell him [tel]	um ihm zu sagen
to see him [siː]	ihn sehen, besuchen

Exercise 7

box [bɒks]	Kasten, Kästchen
I'll be = I will be [aɪl, wɪl]	ich werde sein

Exercise 8

bag [bæg]	Tasche
watch [wɒtʃ]	Armbanduhr
handbag [ˈhændbæg]	Handtasche
to have conversations [kɒnvəˈseɪʃnz]	um Gespräche zu führen
like those above [ðəʊz əˈbʌv]	wie die obigen

Exercise 10

Who is going where?	Wer fährt, reist wohin?
colour [ˈkʌlə]	Farbe
destination [destɪˈneɪʃn]	Ziel(ort)
little [ˈlɪtl]	klein
black [blæk]	schwarz
red [red]	rot
brown [braʊn]	braun
white [waɪt]	weiß
What colour is . . .?	Welche Fabe hat . . .?

London to New York in six seconds

second [ˈsekənd]	Sekunde
month [mʌnθ]	Monat
for six months	sechs Monate (lang)
back [bæk]	zurück
enormous [ɪˈnɔːməs]	riesig, gewaltig
bill [bɪl]	Rechnung
pound (£)	Pfund (englische Währung)
was [wɒz]	war
he wasn't = was not [wɒznt, wɒz ˈnɒt]	er war nicht
surprised [səˈpraɪzd]	überrascht
because [bɪˈkɒz]	weil

had phoned [həd fəʊnd]	hatte angerufen
every ['evrɪ]	jede(r, s, n)
to wake him up [weɪk, ʌp]	um ihn zu wecken
nowadays ['naʊədeɪz]	heutzutage
world [wɜːld]	Welt
all over the world	in der ganzen Welt
fact [fækt]	Tatsache
in fact	tatsächlich, in der Tat
dial direct ['daɪəl dɪ'rekt]	direkt, selbst wählen
almost ['ɔːlməʊst]	beinahe, fast
international [ɪntə'næʃənl]	international
call [kɔːl]	Anruf
wait for [weɪt fə]	warten auf
dialling tone ['daɪəlɪŋ təʊn]	Wählton
code [kəʊd]	Vorwahlnummer
routing number ['ruːtɪŋ nʌmbə]	Ortsnetzkennzahl
subscriber [səb'skraɪbə]	Teilnehmer
note [nəʊt]	beachten
first [fɜːst]	erste(r, s, n)
digit ['dɪdʒɪt]	Ziffer
omit [ə'mɪt]	aus-, weglassen
should be omitted [ʃʊd]	sollte weggelassen werden
live [lɪv]	leben, wohnen
Good night. [gʊd 'naɪt]	Gute Nacht.
when [wen]	wenn
first [fɜːst]	zuerst

Opinions

weekend [wiːk'end]	Wochenende
shopkeeper ['ʃɒpkiːpə]	Geschäftsmann, Ladeninhaber
country cottage ['kɒtɪdʒ]	Landhaus
factory worker ['fæktərɪ 'wɜːkə]	Fabrikarbeiter(in)
nothing special ['nʌθɪŋ 'speʃl]	nichts Besonderes

5. What are your interests?

interest ['ɪntrɪst]	Interesse
talk (to) [tɔːk]	sprechen (mit)
help [help]	helfen
personal ['pɜːsnl]	persönlich
interview ['ɪntəvjuː]	Interview, Gespräch
sit down [sɪt 'daʊn]	sich hinsetzen
smoke [sməʊk]	rauchen
a few [ə 'fjuː]	ein paar

chemical engineer ['kemɪkl endʒɪ'nɪə]	Chemotechniker(in)
sport [spɔːt]	Sport
Yes, I do.	Ja.
judo ['dʒuːdəʊ]	Judo
I see.	Ich verstehe.
much [mʌtʃ]	sehr, viel
ask [ɑːsk]	bitten
certainly ['sɜːtnlɪ]	sicher, gewiß
foreigner ['fɒrɪnə]	Ausländer(in), Fremde(r)
Englishman ['ɪŋglɪʃmən]	Engländer
hot water bottle [hɒt 'wɔːtə bɒtl]	Wärmflasche
alien ['eɪljən]	Fremde(r), Ausländer(in)

How to say it

likes [laɪks]	Vorlieben
dislikes ['dɪslaɪks]	Abneigungen
polite [pə'laɪt]	höflich
No, I don't = do not. [dəʊnt, dʊ 'nɒt]	Nein.
dance [dɑːns]	tanzen
dancing ['dɑːnsɪŋ]	Tanzen
So do I. ['səʊ dʊ 'aɪ]	Ich auch.
Do you? I don't.	Wirklich? Ich nicht.
cooking ['kʊkɪŋ]	Kochen
football ['fʊtbɔːl]	Fußball
swimming ['swɪmɪŋ]	Schwimmen
Don't you? I do.	Sie nicht? Ich ja.
Nor do I. [nɔː dʊ 'aɪ]	Ich auch nicht.
speak (to) [spiːk]	sprechen (mit)
sixty ['sɪkstɪ]	60
seventy ['sevntɪ]	70
eighty ['eɪtɪ]	80
ninety ['naɪntɪ]	90
a million ['mɪljən]	eine Million

Exercise 2

tennis ['tenɪs]	Tennis
skiing ['skiːɪŋ]	Schifahren
eat [iːt]	essen
write down [raɪt 'daʊn]	aufschreiben

Exercise 3

classical ['klæsɪkl]	klassisch
rock music ['rɒk 'mjuːzɪk]	Rockmusik
thriller ['θrɪlə]	Reißer, spannender Film
song contest ['sɒŋ kɒntest]	Schlagerwettbewerb

dinner ['dɪnə] Abendessen
dinner dance Abendgesellschaft mit Tanz

Exercise 4
sports [spɔːts] Sportarten
game [geɪm] Spiel
each [iːtʃ] jede(r, s) (einzelne)
play [pleɪ] spielen
badminton ['bædmɪntən] Federball
golf [gɒlf] Golf
chess [tʃes] Schach
ride [raɪd] reiten
go riding reiten (gehen)
fish [fɪʃ] angeln
go fishing angeln gehen
skate [skeɪt] Schlittschuh laufen
between [bɪ'twiːn] zwischen
spare time ['speə taɪm] Freizeit

Exercise 5
visit ['vɪzɪt] besuchen
museum [mjuː'zɪəm] Museum
church [tʃɜːtʃ] Kirche
art gallery ['ɑːt gælərɪ] Kunstgalerie, -ausstellung
go for walks ['gəʊ fə 'wɔːks] spazierengehen
listen to ['lɪsn tʊ] an-, zuhören
partner ['pɑːtnə] Partner

Exercise 6
holiday ['hɒlədɪ] freier Tag, Ferien
have a holiday Ferien, Urlaub machen
alternative [ɔːl'tɜːnətɪv] Alternative, Möglichkeit zur Wahl

culture ['kʌltʃə] Kultur
go shopping ['ʃɒpɪŋ] einkaufen (gehen)
go sightseeing ['saɪtsiːɪŋ] (die) Sehenswürdigkeiten besichtigen

sail [seɪl] segeln
go sailing segeln gehen

Exercise 7
come in [kʌm 'ɪn] hereinkommen

Exercise 8
across [ə'krɒs] waagerecht
down [daʊn] senkrecht

plane [pleɪn] Flugzeug
train [treɪn] Zug

What is an Englishman?
drink [drɪŋk] trinken
tea [tiː] Tee
strong [strɒŋ] stark
sugar ['ʃʊgə] Zucker
many ['menɪ] viele
prefer [prɪ'fɜː] bevorzugen, es vorziehen
also ['ɔːlsəʊ] auch
spend [spend] ver-, zubringen
a lot [ə 'lɒt] viele, eine Menge
statistics [stə'tɪstɪks] Statistik(en)
house [haʊs] Haus
garden ['gɑːdn] Garten
large [lɑːdʒ] groß
south-east [saʊθ'iːst] Südosten
child, children [tʃaɪld, 'tʃɪldrən] Kind, Kinder
a week [ə 'wiːk] in der Woche
strike [straɪk] Streik
he is on strike er streikt
look after [lʊk 'ɑːftə] sich kümmern um, versorgen

works part time ['pɑːt taɪm] arbeitet halbtags
three weeks' holiday a year [jɜː] (einen) dreiwöchigen Urlaub im Jahr, jährlich
without [wɪ'ðaʊt] ohne
north [nɔːθ] Norden
a forty-hour week eine Vierzigstundenwoche

Opinions
drive [draɪv] Fahrt
car [kɑː] Wagen, Auto
go for a drive in the car einen Ausflug mit dem Auto machen
bus conductor ['bʌs kən'dʌktə] Busschaffner
get up [get 'ʌp] aufstehen

6. Looking after a visitor
visitor ['vɪzɪtə] Besucher(in), Gast
well-known ['wel nəʊn] bekannt
writer ['raɪtə] Schriftsteller(in)

organise [ˈɔːgənaɪz] — organisieren
visit [ˈvɪzɪt] — Besuch
bump into [bʌmp ˈɪntə] — zufällig treffen
at lunch time [ət ˈlʌntʃ taɪm] — zur Mittagszeit, in der Mittagspause

something [ˈsʌmθɪŋ] — etwas
sure [ʃʊə] — sicher
about 45 [əˈbaʊt] — ungefähr 45
does [dʌz] — tut
play the piano [pɪˈænəʊ] — Klavier spielen
expect [ɪkˈspekt] — erwarten, annehmen, vermuten

have a party [ˈpɑːtɪ] — eine Party geben
angel [ˈeɪndʒəl] — Engel

How to say it

stop (at) [stɒp (ət)] — halten (an, bei)
Yes, he does. — Ja.
No, he doesn't = does not. — Nein.
  [ˈdʌznt, dʌz ˈnɒt]
guitar [gɪˈtɑː] — Gitarre
subject [ˈsʌbdʒɪkt] — Subjekt, Satzgegenstand
third [θɜːd] — dritte(r, s)
know [nəʊ] — kennen
not . . . either [ˈaɪðə] — auch nicht

Exercise 3

How old is he, do you think? — Wie alt ist er, glauben Sie?

perhaps [pəˈhæps] — vielleicht

Exercise 4

group [gruːp] — Gruppe
single [ˈsɪŋgl] — alleinstehend, unverheiratet
divorced [dɪˈvɔːst] — geschieden
well [wel] — gut

Exercise 5

activity [ækˈtɪvətɪ] — Aktivität, Tätigkeit

Exercise 6

the West End [ðə ˈwest ˈend] — (vornehme) Gegend Londons
by car [baɪ ˈkɑː] — mit dem Auto
by Underground — mit der U-Bahn
  [ˈʌndəgraʊnd]

silly [ˈsɪlɪ] — albern, lächerlich
instead [ɪnˈsted] — statt dessen
the City [ˈsɪtɪ] — Banken- und Geschäftsviertel Londons

Exercise 7

put it right [raɪt] — stellen Sie es richtig, berichtigen Sie es

goes to watch him play football — geht ihm beim Fußballspielen zusehen

Exercise 8

go by bus — mit dem Bus fahren
usually [ˈjuːʒʊəlɪ] — gewöhnlich
at the garage [ˈgærɑːdʒ] — in der Garage, Werkstatt, an der Tankstelle
which [wɪtʃ] — welche(r, s)
which bus to take — welchen Bus er nehmen soll

Exercise 10

How do you get to . . .? — Wie kommt man nach . . .?
Northern Line [ˈnɔːðən ˈlaɪn] — nördliche Strecke
change to [tʃeɪndʒ] — umsteigen in/auf
central [ˈsentrəl] — mittler(e)
give directions [dɪˈrekʃnz] — Anweisungen geben

Australia

more than [ˈmɔː ðən] — mehr als
kilometre [ˈkɪləʊmiːtə] — Kilometer
it takes [teɪks] — es dauert
to get there — um dorthin zu kommen
by boat [bəʊt] — mit dem Schiff
bigger than [ˈbɪgə ðən] — größer als
population [pɒpjʊˈleɪʃn] — Bevölkerung, Einwohner(zahl)

kangaroo [kæŋgəˈruː] — Känguruh
koala bear [kəʊˈɑːlə beə] — Koalabär
republic [rɪˈpʌblɪk] — Republik
capital [ˈkæpɪtl] — Hauptstadt
develop [dɪˈveləp] — (sich) entwickeln
rather [ˈrɑːðə] — ziemlich
slowly [ˈsləʊlɪ] — langsam
right over — genau gegenüber
side [saɪd] — Seite
air [eə] — Luft
by air — auf dem Luftwege, mit dem Flugzeug

sea [siː] — See

by sea	auf dem Seewege, mit dem Schiff
nearly ['nɪəlɪ]	beinahe
as big as [əz 'bɪg əz]	so groß wie
only ['əʊnlɪ]	nur
compared with [kəm'peəd wɪð]	verglichen mit, im Vergleich zu
winter ['wɪntə]	Winter
summer ['sʌmə]	Sommer
vice versa ['vaɪs 'vɜ:sə]	umgekehrt
strange [streɪndʒ]	seltsam, fremd(artig)
animal ['ænɪml]	Tier
recognize ['rekəgnaɪz]	anerkennen
Queen Elisabeth [kwi:n ɪ'lɪzəbəθ]	Königin Elisabeth
Head of State ['hed əv 'steɪt]	Staatsoberhaupt
fast [fɑ:st]	schnell
powerful ['paʊəfʊl]	mächtig, stark
by the year 2,000	bis zum Jahre 2000

Opinions

sort of ['sɔ:t əv]	Art, Sorte von
pensioner ['penʃənə]	Pensionär(in), Rentner(in)
accordion [ə'kɔ:djən]	Ziehharmonika, Akkordeon

7. A trip to Oxford

trip [trɪp]	Ausflug, Kurzreise
she is going to	sie wird
way [weɪ]	Art, Weise
the best way	am besten
car hire ['haɪə]	Autovermietung
How much is that? [mʌtʃ]	Was kostet das?
it depends [dɪ'pendz]	es kommt darauf an
a day	am Tag
return [rɪ'tɜ:n]	(hin und) zurück
get [get]	besorgen
Okay. [əʊ'keɪ]	In Ordnung.
Thank goodness! ['θæŋk 'gʊdnɪs]	Gott sei Dank!

How to say it

plan [plæn]	planen
planning ['plænɪŋ]	Planen, Pläne machen
decide [dɪ'saɪd]	sich entscheiden, beschließen

send [send]	schicken
letter ['letə]	Brief
postcard ['pəʊstkɑ:d]	Postkarte
abroad [ə'brɔ:d]	ins Ausland
pence (p) [pens, pi:]	Pence (englische Währung)

Exercise 1

picnic ['pɪknɪk]	Picknick

Exercise 2

library ['laɪbrərɪ]	Bücherei, Bibliothek

Exercise 4

transport ['trænspɔ:t]	Transport, Verkehr(smittel)
air terminal	Haltestelle für Flughafenbus
railway station ['reɪlweɪ 'steɪʃn]	Bahnhof
taxi rank ['tæksɪ ræŋk]	Taxistand
harbour ['hɑ:bə]	Hafen

Exercise 5

hire ['haɪə]	mieten; Miete
latest ['leɪtɪst]	neueste(r, s)
model ['mɒdl]	Modell
luxury ['lʌkʃərɪ]	Luxus
sports car ['spɔ:ts kɑ:]	Sportwagen
following ['fɒləʊɪŋ]	folgende(r, s)
rate [reɪt]	Gebühr, Preis
include [ɪn'klu:d]	einschließen, umfassen
full insurance [fʊl ɪn'ʃʊərəns]	volle Versicherung, Vollkasko
mile [maɪl]	Meile (= 1,6 km)
free [fri:]	frei, kostenlos
mileage ['maɪlɪdʒ]	Kilometerstand, -zahl
500 miles free mileage	die ersten 800 km sind frei
return [rɪ'tɜ:n]	zurückbringen
must be returned	müssen zurückgebracht werden
by midnight ['mɪdnaɪt]	bis Mitternacht
last [lɑ:st]	letzte(r, s)

Exercise 6

madam ['mædəm]	gnädige Frau

Exercise 8

gap [gæp] — Lücke
au pair (girl) [əʊ 'peə] — Aupair-Mädchen
wish you were here [wɪʃ, wə] — ich wünschte, du wärest hier
next [nekst] — nächste(r, s)
Love, [lʌv] — Herzlich(e Grüße),
c/o = care of ['keə əv] — per Adresse, bei

Exercise 10

order ['ɔ:də] — Reihenfolge

A letter

two years ago [ə'gəʊ] — vor zwei Jahren
Dear June, [dɪə] — Liebe June,
clean [kli:n] — reinigen, säubern
clean the house — saubermachen
do the shopping ['ʃɒpɪŋ] — einkaufen (gehen), die Einkäufe machen
do the cooking ['kʊkɪŋ] — kochen
lessons ['lesnz] — Unterricht
just one thing [dʒʌst] — nur eins
for hours [fər 'aʊəz] — stundenlang
be homesick ['həʊmsɪk] — an Heimweh leiden
teach [ti:tʃ] — lehren, beibringen
reverse [rɪ'vɜ:s] — umkehren, umdrehen
charge [tʃɑ:dʒ] — Kosten
reverse the charges — Gebühren zahlt der Angerufene
stop [stɒp] — aufhören, Schluß machen
Best wishes, ['wɪʃɪz] — Mit den besten Grüßen,
terrace ['terəs] — Terrasse, Panoramaweg
classes ['klɑ:sɪz] — Unterricht
wants her to pay [wɒnts, peɪ] — möchte, daß sie bezahlt

Opinions

district nurse ['dɪstrɪkt nɜ:s] — Bezirkskrankenschwester
fisherman ['fɪʃəmən] — Fischer
librarian [laɪ'breərɪən] — Bibliothekar(in)
walk [wɔ:k] — (zu Fuß) gehen

8. Where would you like to go?

arrange [ə'reɪndʒ] — arrangieren, veranstalten
tour [tʊə] — Tour, (Rund-)Reise, -Fahrt
sightseeing tour ['saɪtsi:ɪŋ] — Besichtigungsfahrt

coast [kəʊst] — Küste
book [bʊk] — buchen, bestellen
service ['sɜ:vɪs] — Dienst(leistung)
at your service — zu Ihren Diensten
round [raʊnd] — rund (um)
round London — durch London
further ['fɜ:ðə] — weitere
detail ['di:teɪl] — Detail, Einzelheit
that's no good — das geht nicht
I'm afraid [ə'freɪd] — fürchte ich

How to say it

I'm going on holiday ['hɒlədɪ] — ich gehe, fahre auf Urlaub
business trip ['bɪznɪs trɪp] — Geschäftsreise
where to? [weə 'tu:] — wohin?
tell the time [taɪm] — sagen, wie spät es ist
give a light [laɪt] — Feuer geben
start (work) [stɑ:t (wɜ:k)] — (mit der Arbeit) anfangen, beginnen
a quarter to/past [ə 'kwɔ:tə tʊ, pɑ:st] — viertel vor/nach
meeting ['mi:tɪŋ] — Besprechung, Treffen

Exercise 1

rain [reɪn] — regnen

Exercise 2

map [mæp] — (Land-)Karte

Exercise 3

committee [kə'mɪtɪ] — Komitee, Ausschuß
sales conference ['seɪlz 'kɒnfərəns] — Verkaufskonferenz

Exercise 5

time-table ['taɪmteɪbl] — Fahrplan
change [tʃeɪndʒ] — umsteigen
clerk [klɑ:k] — Schalterbeamter, -beamtin

The Englishman, the Irishman, the Welshman and the Scotsman

die [daɪ] — sterben
funeral ['fju:nərəl] — Begräbnis
coffin ['kɒfɪn] — Sarg
go down — versenkt werden

perfect ['pɜ:fɪkt]	perfekt
gentleman ['dʒentlmən]	Gentleman, Herr
owe [əʊ]	schulden, schuldig sein
note [nəʊt]	(Bank-)Note, (Geld-) Schein
cheque (book) [tʃek (bʊk)]	Scheck(buch)
pen [pen]	Füller, Kugelschreiber
write out [raɪt 'aʊt]	ausschreiben
pick up [pɪk 'ʌp]	(auf-)nehmen

Opinions

(car) salesman ['seɪlzmən]	(Auto-)Verkäufer
to tour [tʊə]	bereisen, fahren durch
art (student) ['ɑ:t ('stju:dnt)]	Kunst(student, -in)
hitch-hike ['hɪtʃhaɪk]	per Anhalter reisen
round [raʊnd]	durch (ganz)
plumber ['plʌmə]	Installateur, Klempner

9. A new flat

stand [stænd]	stehen
to let [let]	zu vermieten
bureau ['bjʊərəʊ]	Büro
hear [hɪə]	hören
handy ['hændɪ]	praktisch, bequem
What's it like?	Wie ist es?
kitchen ['kɪtʃɪn]	Küche
bathroom ['bɑ:θrʊm]	Bad(ezimmer)
floor [flɔ:]	Etage, Geschoß
on the first floor	im ersten Stock
block of flats ['blɒk əv 'flæts]	Wohnblock
quite [kwaɪt]	ganz, ziemlich
actually ['æktʃʊəlɪ]	tatsächlich, eigentlich
a bit [ə 'bɪt]	etwas, ein wenig
still [stɪl]	doch, trotzdem
near [nɪə]	nahe, in der Nähe von
the best thing about it [θɪŋ]	das beste daran
There's no place like home.	Zuhause ist es doch am besten.

How to say it

bedroom ['bedrʊm]	Schlafzimmer
toilet ['tɔɪlɪt]	Toilette, WC
glasses ['glɑ:sɪz]	Spiegel
upstairs [ʌp'steəz]	oben, im ersten Stock

on the right [raɪt]	rechts, auf der rechten Seite
comfortable ['kʌmfətəbl]	bequem
modern ['mɒdən]	modern
old-fashioned [əʊld'fæʃnd]	altmodisch, unmodern
preposition [prepə'zɪʃn]	Präposition, Verhältnis- wort
cupboard ['kʌbəd]	Schrank
corner ['kɔ:nə]	Ecke
floor [flɔ:]	Fußboden
table ['teɪbl]	Tisch
shopping centre ['ʃɒpɪŋ sentə]	Einkaufszentrum

Exercise 2

bed-sitting room ['bed sɪtɪŋ 'ru:m]	Wohnschlafzimmer

Exercise 4

furniture ['fɜ:nɪtʃə]	Möbel
piece [pi:s]	Stück
piece of furniture	Möbelstück
chair [tʃeə]	Stuhl
sofa ['səʊfə]	Sofa
armchair [ɑ:m'tʃeə]	Sessel
chest of drawers ['tʃest əv 'drɔ:z]	Kommode
coffee table ['kɒfɪ teɪbl]	Couchtisch
bookcase ['bʊkkeɪs]	Bücherschrank, -regal
lamp [læmp]	Lampe

Exercise 5

bed-sitter ['bedsɪtə]	Wohnschlafzimmer, Ein- zimmerwohnung
quiet ['kwaɪət]	ruhig
opposite ['ɒpəzɪt]	gegenüber
along [ə'lɒŋ]	entlang, an
wall [wɔ:l]	Wand
carpet ['kɑ:pɪt]	Teppich
a sort of ['sɔ:t əv]	eine Art
light green [laɪt 'gri:n]	hellgrün
lake [leɪk]	See
window ['wɪndəʊ]	Fenster
really ['rɪəlɪ]	tatsächlich, in der Tat
shower ['ʃaʊə]	Dusche
by the door [dɔ:]	an, neben der Tür

Exercise 6

draw [drɔ:]	zeichnen
bed [bed]	Bett
balcony ['bælkənɪ]	Balkon
left [left]	links
right [raɪt]	rechts

Exercise 7

ask the way ['ɑːsk ðə 'weɪ]	nach dem Weg fragen
police station [pə'liːs steɪʃn]	Polizeirevier, -wache
travel agents ['trævl eɪdʒənts]	Reisebüro

Exercise 8

second ['sekənd]	zweite(r, s)

Exercise 9

couple ['kʌpl]	Paar
host [həʊst]	Gastgeber
hostess ['həʊstɪs]	Gastgeberin
sit [sɪt]	sitzen

The housing problem

housing ['haʊzɪŋ]	Wohnungs-
proper ['prɒpə]	richtig, ordentlich
homeless ['həʊmlɪs]	obdachlos
big city ['sɪtɪ]	Großstadt
sometimes ['sʌmtaɪmz]	mànchmal
probably ['prɒbəblɪ]	wahrscheinlich
the same [seɪm]	die gleiche(n), gleich
everywhere ['evrɪweə]	überall
overcrowding [əʊvə'kraʊdɪŋ]	Überbevökerung
slum [slʌm]	Elendsviertel
high [haɪ]	hoch, hohe(r, s)
rent [rent]	Miete

Opinions

town planning ['taʊn plænɪŋ]	Stadtplanung
district ['dɪstrɪkt]	Bezirk, Wohngegend
mechanic [mɪ'kænɪk]	Mechaniker, Monteur
enough [ɪ'nʌf]	genug, ausreichend
not enough	nicht genügend
architect ['ɑːkɪtekt]	Architekt
park [pɑːk]	Park
overcrowded [əʊvə'kraʊdɪd]	überfüllt
all the same ['ɔːl ðə 'seɪm]	trotz(alle)dem

10. He's a nice man

manager ['mænɪdʒə]	Chef, Direktor
I should think [ʃʊd 'θɪŋk]	denke ich
first name	Vorname
What does she look like?	Wie sieht sie aus?
smart [smɑːt]	modisch, fesch, schick, elegant
type [taɪp]	Typ
women pl. of woman ['wɪmɪn, 'wʊmən]	Frau(en)
men pl. of man [men, mæn]	Mann, Männer
you are all the same	ihr seid alle gleich

How to say it

describe [dɪ'skraɪb]	beschreiben
attractive [ə'træktɪv]	attraktiv, hübsch
lively ['laɪvlɪ]	lebhaft
early ['ɜːlɪ]	früh, zeitig

Exercise 1

dear [dɪə]	Liebling
I don't think Susan's coming	Ich glaube nicht, daß Susan kommt

Exercise 2

slim [slɪm]	schlank
glasses ['glɑːsɪz]	Brille
dark [dɑːk]	dunkel
hair [heə]	Haar(e)
fair [feə]	blond, hell
beard [bɪəd]	Bart
moustache [mə'stɑːʃ]	Schnurrbart
tours manager ['tʊəz mænɪdʒə]	Reiseleiter(in)
short [ʃɔːt]	kurz, klein, untersetzt
tall [tɔːl]	groß
accountant [ə'kaʊntənt]	Buchhalter
bald [bɔːld]	kahl, mit Glatze
caretaker ['keəteɪkə]	Hauswart, -meister
fat [fæt]	dick, korpulent

Exercise 3

look for ['lʊk fə]	suchen

Exercise 4

description [dɪs'krɪpʃn]	Beschreibung
color Am. = colour ['kʌlə]	Farbe

gray Am. = grey [greɪ]	grau
eye [aɪ]	Auge
height [haɪt]	(Körper-)Größe
cms = centimetres ['sentɪmi:təz]	Zentimeter
feature ['fi:tʃə]	Kennzeichen

Exercise 5

clothes [kləʊðz]	Kleider, Kleidung
own [əʊn]	eigen
advertisement [əd'vɜ:tɪsmənt]	Anzeige
choose [tʃu:z]	(aus-)wählen, aussuchen
suit [su:t]	Anzug
jacket ['dʒækɪt]	Jacke, Jackett
trousers ['traʊzəz]	Hose
jeans [dʒi:nz]	Jeans
sweater ['swetə]	Pullover
dress [dres]	Kleid
skirt [skɜ:t]	Rock
blouse [blaʊz]	Bluse
yellow ['jeləʊ]	gelb
shirt [ʃɜ:t]	Hemd
tie [taɪ]	Binder, Schlips
a pair of shoes [peərəv 'ʃu:z]	ein Paar Schuhe

Exercise 6

age [eɪdʒ]	Alter
blonde [blɒnd]	blond
blue [blu:]	blau
build [bɪld]	Körperbau, Statur
report [rɪ'pɔ:t]	melden
reported missing by [rɪ'pɔ:tɪd 'mɪsɪŋ baɪ]	als vermißt gemeldet von
result [rɪ'zʌlt]	Resultat, Ergebnis

Exercise 7

intelligent [ɪn'telɪdʒənt]	intelligent

Exercise 8

are used [ju:zd]	werden gebraucht
chap [tʃæp]	Kerl
programme ['prəʊgræm]	Programm

A question of language

language ['læŋgwɪdʒ]	Sprache
one-eyed ['wʌn aɪd]	einsam
order ['ɔ:də]	bestellen

chocolate ['tʃɒkələt]	Schokolade
biscuit ['bɪskɪt]	Plätzchen, Keks
cigar [sɪ'gɑ:]	Zigarre
mouth [maʊθ]	Mund
turn round [tɜ:n 'raʊnd]	sich umdrehen
smile [smaɪl]	Lächeln
Gee [dʒi:]	Herrje
it sure is great [ʃʊə, greɪt]	das ist ja wirklich prima, großartig
look up [lʊk 'ʌp]	aufblicken
reply [rɪ'plaɪ]	antworten
sir [sɜ:]	mein Herr
mine [maɪn]	mein(e)
they say	man sagt
divide [dɪ'vaɪd]	teilen, trennen
divided by	die getrennt sind durch
glad [glæd]	froh
to hear English spoken ['spəʊkən]	Englisch sprechen zu hören
understand [ʌndə'stænd]	verstehen
each other	sich (gegenseitig)

Opinions

smoking ['sməʊkɪŋ]	(das) Rauchen
script girl ['skrɪpt gɜ:l]	Scriptgirl, Ateliersekretärin
many times ['menɪ 'taɪmz]	viele Male, oft
journalist ['dʒɜ:nəlɪst]	Journalist(in)
should [ʃʊd]	sollte(n)
at work [ət 'wɜ:k]	bei der Arbeit

11. What are you doing at the weekend?

call [kɔ:l]	nennen, rufen
you see	sehen Sie
Monique and me	Monique und ich
Would you like to come, too?	Möchten Sie (auch) mitkommen?
kind [kaɪnd]	freundlich
I'd like to very much	ich möchte sehr gern
Shall I give her a call? [ʃæl]	Soll ich sie (mal) anrufen?
Yes, do.	Ja, unbedingt.
ring [rɪŋ]	(jemanden) anrufen
What a pity! ['wɒt ə 'pɪtɪ]	Wie schade!
another time [ə'nʌðə]	ein andermal
hope [həʊp]	hoffen
sure [ʃʊə]	sicher, gewiß

love [lʌv]	lieben
I'd love to	Ich würde sehr gern

How to say it

invite [ɪn'vaɪt]	einladen
invitation [ɪnvɪ'teɪʃn]	Einladung
Let's see.	Laß mal sehen.
go away [ə'weɪ]	wegfahren
on business ['bɪznɪs]	geschäftlich
January ['dʒænjʊərɪ]	Januar
February ['februərɪ]	Februar
March [mɑ:tʃ]	März
April ['eɪprəl]	April
May [meɪ]	Mai
June [dʒu:n]	Juni
July [dʒʊ'laɪ]	Juli
August ['ɔ:gəst]	August
September [sep'tembə]	September
October [ɒk'təʊbə]	Oktober
November [nəʊ'vembə]	November
December [dɪ'sembə]	Dezember
spring [sprɪŋ]	Frühling
autumn ['ɔ:təm]	Herbst

Exercise 1

baby-sit ['beɪbɪsɪt]	auf das Baby aufpassen

Exercise 2

course [kɔ:s]	Kurs
school [sku:l]	Schule
school meeting	Elternversammlung

Exercise 3

Look,	Hör mal,
hold on [həʊld 'ɒn]	am Apparat bleiben
hold on a minute	wart mal einen Moment
Oh, well	Na, gut
see if	sehen ob

Exercise 6

at last [ət 'lɑ:st]	endlich
earth [ɜ:θ]	Erde
Where on earth	wo um Himmels willen
drawer ['drɔ:ə]	Schub(fach)
top [tɒp]	oberste(r, s)
the top one [ðə 'tɒp wʌn]	der, die, das oberste
pocket ['pɒkɪt]	Tasche

Exercise 7

socks [sɒks]	Socken

Exercise 9

market ['mɑ:kɪt]	Markt
hospital ['hɒspɪtl]	Krankenhaus

Brighton by the sea

by the sea	an der See
the east coast ['i:st kəʊst]	die Ostküste
university [ju:nɪ'vɜ:sɪtɪ]	Universität
seaside ['si:saɪd]	See-, Meeresküste
seaside town	Seebad, Badeort
south coast ['saʊθ kəʊst]	Südküste
south of ['saʊθ əv]	südlich von
coffee house	Kaffeehaus, Café
administrative	Verwaltungs-
[əd'mɪnɪstrətɪv]	
cultural ['kʌltʃrəl]	kulturell, Kultur-
just [dʒʌst]	gerade
outside [aʊt'saɪd]	außerhalb
technical college ['teknɪkl	technische Fachhoch-
'kɒlɪdʒ]	schule
several ['sevrəl]	mehrere
dozen ['dʌzn]	Dutzend
dozens of	Dutzende von
century ['sentʃərɪ]	Jahrhundert
palace ['pælɪs]	Palast, Schloß
king [kɪŋ]	König
enjoy [ɪn'dʒɔɪ]	genießen
at the same time	gleichzeitig

Opinions

shop manager	Geschäftsführer
retired [rɪ'taɪəd]	pensioniert, im Ruhestand
sailor ['seɪlə]	Seemann, Matrose
are fun [fʌn]	machen Spaß
guest [gest]	Gast

12. Can I get you anything?

anything ['enɪθɪŋ]	(irgend) etwas
Can I get you anything?	Kann ich dir was mitbringen, besorgen?
I'm just going to the shops.	Ich gehe eben mal einkaufen.

packet ['pækɪt]   Päckchen
What sort?   Welche Sorte? Was für welche?

anything else [els]   etwas anderes, noch etwas

mind [maɪnd]   beachten
never mind   (das) macht nichts
menu ['menjuː]   Speisekarte
fried fish [fraɪd 'fɪʃ]   Bratfisch
roast [rəʊst]   braten, rösten
roast beef ['rəʊst biːf]   Rinderbraten
ham salad ['hæm 'sæləd]   Schinkensalat
lasagne [la'sanjə]   überbackene Nudeln mit Fleischsauce

What are you going to have?   Was nimmst du?
wave [weɪv]   winken
She's waving to you.   Sie winkt dir zu.
exactly [ɪg'zæktlɪ]   genau
not exactly   eigentlich nicht, nicht gerade

she's coming over   sie kommt herüber
you English   ihr Engländer
company ['kʌmpənɪ]   Gesellschaft
crowd [kraʊd]   (Menschen-)Menge

How to say it

asking for something   um etwas bitten
offer ['ɒfə]   anbieten
the chemist's ['kemɪsts]   die Apotheke
supermarket ['suːpəmaːkɪt]   Supermarkt
match [mætʃ]   Streichholz
a box of matches   eine Schachtel Streichhölzer

a bottle of shampoo [ʃæm'puː]   eine Flasche Haarwaschmittel
a kilo of coffee ['kiːləʊ]   ein Kilo Kaffee
ice-cream [aɪs'kriːm]   Speiseeis

Exercise 1

they haven't got any ['enɪ]   sie haben kein(e)
boss [bɒs]   Chef

Exercise 2

correct [kə'rekt]   richtig
can [kæn]   Dose, Büchse
bar [baː]   Tafel, Stück
a bar of chocolate   eine Tafel Schokolade
chocolates ['tʃɒkələts]   Pralinen

a box of chocolates   eine Schachtel, ein Kasten Konfekt

aspirin ['æspərɪn]   Aspirin
nut [nʌt]   Nuß
soap [səʊp]   Seife
sherry ['ʃerɪ]   Sherry

Exercise 3

shopping list ['ʃɒpɪŋ lɪst]   Einkaufsliste, -zettel
eight-penny ['eɪtpenɪ]   Acht-Pence-
stamp [stæmp]   (Brief-)Marke
paper shop ['peɪpə ʃɒp]   Zeitungsladen
local paper ['ləʊkl 'peɪpə]   Lokalzeitung
corn flakes ['kɔːnfleɪks]   Cornflakes
cash a cheque [kæʃ ə 'tʃek]   einen Scheck einlösen
Where do you get cigarettes?   Wo bekommt man Zigaretten?

Exercise 6

tea shop ['tiːʃɒp]   Teestube
cat [kæt]   Katze
per person [pə 'pɜːsn]   pro Person
10p = 10 pence [piː, pens]   10 Pence (englische Währung)

glass [glaːs]   Glas
sandwich ['sænwɪdʒ]   Sandwich, belegtes Weißbrot

cheese [tʃiːz]   Käse
tomato [tə'maːtəʊ]   Tomate
egg [eg]   Ei
cakes [keɪks]   Kuchen(stücke)
portion ['pɔːʃn]   Portion, Stück
fruit [fruːt]   Obst, Früchte
Danish pastry ['deɪnɪʃ 'peɪstrɪ]   Blätterteiggebäck
would be nice [wʊd]   wäre (ganz) schön

Exercise 8

shopping ['ʃɒpɪŋ]   Einkauf
cost [kɒst]   kosten
fruit salad [fruːt 'sæləd]   Obstsalat
orange juice ['ɒrɪndʒ dʒuːs]   Orangensaft
soup [suːp]   Suppe
instant ['ɪnstənt]   sofort löslich
instant coffee   Pulverkaffee
Cheddar cheese ['tʃedə]   Cheddar-Käse
potato [pə'teɪtəʊ]   Kartoffel
apple ['æpl]   Apfel
banana [bə'naːnə]   Banane

pork chop ['pɔːk tʃɒp]	Schweinekotelet
shrimp [ʃrɪmp]	Garnele, Krabbe
hecto ['hektəʊ]	100 g
white bread [bred]	Weißbrot
crisp [krɪsp]	knusprig
crisp bread	Knäckebrot

Silly stories

silly ['sɪlɪ]	albern
story ['stɔːrɪ]	Geschichte
remember [rɪ'membə]	(sich) erinnern, einprägen
fly [flaɪ]	Fliege
dead [ded]	tot
don't worry ['wʌrɪ]	machen Sie sich keine Sorgen, seien Sie beruhigt
charge [tʃɑːdʒ]	Kosten
there's no extra charge ['ekstrə]	es wird nicht extra berechnet
swim [swɪm]	schwimmen
loud [laʊd]	laut
will want one [wɒnt]	wird eine haben wollen
spider ['spaɪdə]	Spinne
tiger ['taɪgə]	Tiger
steak [steɪk]	Steak, Filet
when [wen]	als
funny ['fʌnɪ]	spaßig, komisch
elephant ['elɪfənt]	Elefant
ear [ɪə]	Ohr
crocodile ['krɒkədaɪl]	Krokodil
foot, feet [fʊt, fiːt]	Fuß, Füße
joke [dʒəʊk]	Witz, Scherz
rare [reə]	blutig
medium ['miːdjəm]	mittel, rosa
well-done [wel'dʌn]	(gut) durchgebraten
plate [pleɪt]	Teller
joke [dʒəʊk]	scherzen, Witze machen
you must be joking	Sie machen (bestimmt) Witze
cut out [kʌt 'aʊt]	herausschneiden
sweets [swiːts]	Nachspeisen, -tisch
mermaid ['mɜːmeɪd]	Seejungfrau
tail [teɪl]	Schwanz
toast [təʊst]	Toast
he says to himself [sez tə hɪm'self]	er sagt zu sich (selbst)
that can't be right	das kann nicht stimmen
without any surprise [sə'praɪz]	ohne jede Überraschung
worried ['wʌrɪd]	beunruhigt

terrible ['terəbl]	furchtbar, schrecklich
I'm terribly sorry	es tut mir furchtbar leid
happen ['hæpən]	passieren, geschehen
bread [bred]	(Weiß-)Brot

Opinions

bachelor ['bætʃələ]	Junggeselle
artist ['ɑːtɪst]	Künstler(in)
you get better service ['sɜːvɪs]	man wird besser bedient

13. Would you like some coffee?

cafeteria [kæfɪ'tɪərɪə]	Cafeteria, Imbißstube
assistant [ə'sɪstənt]	Assistent (in)
yours [jɔːz]	deine(r, s)
Can I give you a lift?	Kann ich Sie (im Auto) mitnehmen?
pick up [pɪk 'ʌp]	abholen
Let's all have lunch together, shall we?	Wollen wir alle zusammen Mittag essen (gehen)?

How to say it

method ['meθəd]	Methode, Art und Weise
beside [bɪ'saɪd]	neben
behind [bɪ'haɪnd]	hinter
in front of [ɪn 'frʌnt əv]	vor
clock [klɒk]	Uhr

Exercise 1

ashtray ['æʃtreɪ]	Aschenbecher
bin [bɪn]	Abfallkorb, -eimer
counter ['kaʊntə]	Theke
fruit machine ['fruːt məʃiːn]	Spielautomat
plant [plɑːnt]	Pflanze
radiator ['reɪdɪeɪtə]	Heizkörper
tray [treɪ]	Tablett

Exercise 2

anywhere ['enɪweə]	irgendwo

Exercise 4

princess ['prɪnses]	Prinzessin
prince [prɪns]	Prinz
poker ['pəʊkə]	Poker
Be careful ['keəfʊl]	Sei vorsichtig! Sieh dich vor!

Alphabetische Wortliste

Die Ziffern geben an, in welcher *Unit* das Wort in dieser Bedeutung zum ersten Male vorkommt.
Personen- und Ortsnamen siehe S. 141, Ländernamen und davon abgeleitete Wörter siehe S. 138.

a

a [ə] ein(e) 1; pro 7
about [ə'baʊt] über 1; ungefähr 6
above [ə'bʌv] über, oben 1
abroad [ə'brɔːd] ins Ausland 7
academy [ə'kædəmɪ] Akademie 3
accordion [ə'kɔːdjən] Akkordeon 6
accountant [ə'kaʊntənt]
  Buchhalter 10
across [ə'krɒs] waagerecht 5
activity [æk'tɪvətɪ] Tätigkeit 6
actually ['æktʃʊəlɪ] tatsächlich 9
address [ə'dres] Adresse, Anschrift 1
administrative [əd'mɪnɪstrətɪv]
  Verwaltungs- 11
advertisement [əd'vɜːtɪsmənt]
  Anzeige 10
AF = Air France ['eɪ'ef, eə 'frɑːns] 4
afraid [ə'freɪd] bange 8
  I'm afraid ich fürchte, leider 8
after ['ɑːftə] nach 1
afternoon [ɑːftə'nuːn] Nachmittag 2
again [ə'gen] wieder 1
age [eɪdʒ] Alter 10
ago [ə'gəʊ] vor 7
air [eə] Luft 6
  by air mit dem Flugzeug 6
airline ['eəlaɪn] Fluggesellschaft 1
airport ['eəpɔːt] Flughafen 1
air terminal ['eə tɜːmɪnl] Haltestelle für
  Flughafenbus 1
alien ['eɪljən] Fremde(r),
  Ausländer(in) 5
all [ɔːl] alle 1
all over the world ['ɔːl əʊvə ðə 'wɜːld]
  in der ganzen Welt 4
all right ['ɔːl 'raɪt] gut, in Ordnung 1
allowance [ə'laʊəns] erlaubte
  Menge 1
almost ['ɔːlməʊst] fast, beinahe 4
along [ə'lɒŋ] entlang, an 9
also ['ɔːlsəʊ] auch 5
alternative [ɔːl'tɜːnətɪv] Alternative 5

am [æm, əm] bin 1
a.m. ['eɪ'em] vormittags 3
an [ən] ein(e) 1
and [ənd] und 1
angel ['eɪndʒəl] Engel 6
animal ['ænɪml] Tier 6
another [ə'nʌðə] noch ein, ein
  anderer 1
answer ['ɑːnsə] Antwort 1;
  antworten 1
any ['enɪ] irgendein(e) 3
  not . . . any kein 12
anything ['enɪθɪŋ] irgend etwas 12
anywhere ['enɪweə] irgendwo 13
apple ['æpl] Apfel 12
April ['eɪprəl] April 11
architect ['ɑːkɪtekt] Architekt 9
are [ɑː] bist, seid, sind 1
armchair [ɑːm'tʃeə] Sessel 9
arrange [ə'reɪndʒ] verabreden 2;
  arrangieren 8
art [ɑːt] Kunst 8
art gallery ['ɑːt gælərɪ] Kunstgalerie 5
artist ['ɑːtɪst] Künstler(in) 12
as [æz] als 1
as . . . as [əz . . . əz] so . . . wie 6
ashtray ['æʃtreɪ] Aschenbecher 13
ask [ɑːsk] fragen 3; bitten 5
  ask for bitten um 2
aspirin ['æspərɪn] Aspirin 12
assistant [ə'sɪstənt] Assistent(in) 13
  assistant manager Chefassistent 1
at [ət] an, in, bei, auf 1
atmosphere ['ætməsfɪə]
  Atmosphäre 3
attractive [ə'træktɪv] hübsch 10
August ['ɔːgəst] August 11
au pair (girl) [əʊ 'peə (gɜːl)]
  Aupair-Mädchen 7
autumm ['ɔːtəm] Herbst 11
awful ['ɔːfʊl] furchtbar, schrecklich 2

b

BA = British Airways ['biː'eɪ, 'brɪtɪʃ
  'eəweɪz] 1
baby-sit ['beɪbɪsɪt] auf das Baby
  aufpassen 11
bachelor ['bætʃələ] Junggeselle 12
back [bæk] zurück 1
bad [bæd] schlecht 3
badminton ['bædmɪntən] Federball 5
bag [bæg] Tasche 4
balcony ['bælkənɪ] Balkon 9
bald [bɔːld] kahl 10
banana [bə'nɑːnə] Banane 12
band wagon ['bænd wægən] Wagen
  mit Musikkapelle 3
bank [bæŋk] Bank 1
bank clerk ['bæŋk klɑːk]
  Bankangestellte(r) 1
bar [bɑː] Tafel, Stück 12
bathroom ['bɑːθrʊm] Bad(ezimmer) 9
be [biː] sein 4
beard [bɪəd] Bart 10
beautiful ['bjuːtəfʊl] schön 2
because [bɪ'kɒz] weil 4
bed [bed] Bett 9
bedroom ['bedrʊm] Schlafzimmer 9
bed-sitter, bed-sitting room ['bedsɪtə,
  'bedsɪtɪŋ rʊm] Wohnschlafzimmer 9
beer [bɪə] Bier 2
before [bɪ'fɔː] vor 1
behind [bɪ'haɪnd] hinter 13
below [bɪ'ləʊ] unter 2
beside [bɪ'saɪd] neben 13
best [best] (am) besten 2
better ['betə] besser 1
between [bɪ'twiːn] zwischen 5
big [bɪg] groß 6
big city [bɪg 'sɪtɪ] Großstadt 9
bill [bɪl] Rechnung 4
bin [bɪn] Abfallkorb, -eimer 13
birth [bɜːθ] Geburt 1
biscuit ['bɪskɪt] Plätzchen, Keks 10
bit [bɪt] Stück 9

black [blæk] schwarz 4

block of flats ['blɒk əv 'flæts] Wohnblock 9

block letters ['blɒk letəz] Druckbuchstaben 1

blonde [blɒnd] blond 10

blouse [blaʊz] Bluse 10

blue [bluː] blau 10

boat [bəʊt] Boot, Schiff 6

book [bʊk] Buch 3; buchen 8

bookcase ['bʊkkeɪs] Bücherschrank, -regal 9

boss [bɒs] chef 12

both [bəʊθ] beide 1

bottle ['bɒtl] Flasche 1

  a bottle of whisky eine Flasche Whisky 1

box [bɒks] Schachtel, Kasten, Kästchen 4

boy [bɔɪ] Junge 1

boyfriend ['bɔɪfrend] Freund 2

bread [bred] Brot 12

bring in(to) [brɪŋ 'ɪn(tʊ)] einführen 1

brown [braʊn] braun 4

brochure ['brəʊʃə] Prospekt 1

brother ['brʌðə] Bruder 3

build [bɪld] Körperbau, Statur 10

bump into ['bʌmp ɪntʊ] zufällig treffen 6

bureau ['bjʊərəʊ] Büro 9

bus [bʌs] (Linien-)Bus 4

bus conductor ['bʌs kən'dʌktə] Busschaffner 5

bus driver ['bʌs draɪvə] Busfahrer 1

bus stop ['bʌs stɒp] (Bus-)Haltestelle 2

business ['bɪznɪs] Geschäft 11

  on bussiness geschäftlich 11

bussiness man ['bɪznɪsmən] Geschäftsmann 1

business trip ['bɪznɪs trɪp] Geschäftsreise 8

but [bʌt] aber 2

butter ['bʌtə] Butter 12

by [baɪ] mit 6; bis 6; bei 9; an 11

bye [baɪ] tschüs 4

bye-bye [baɪ'baɪ] (auf) Wiedersehn 4

C

cafeteria [kæfɪ'tɪərɪə] Cafeteria 13

cake [keɪk] Kuchen 12

call [kɔːl] nennen 2; anrufen 4; Anruf 4

  be called [bɪ 'kɔːld] genannt werden 2

can [kæn, kən] können 1

can [kæn] Büchse, Dose 12

capital ['kæpɪtl] Hauptstadt 6

car [kɑː] Wagen, Auto 5

card [kɑːd] (Visiten-)Karte 1

careful ['keəfʊl] sorgfältig 13

caretaker ['keəteɪkə] Hauswart, -meister 10

car hire ['kɑː haɪə] Autovermietung 7

carpet ['kɑːpɪt] Teppich 9

cash a cheque ['kæʃ ə 'tʃek] einen Scheck einlösen 12

cat [kæt] Katze 1

central ['sentrəl] zentral 6

centre ['sentə] Zentrum, Mitte 1

century ['sentʃərɪ] Jahrhundert 11

certainly ['sɜːtnlɪ] gewiß, sicher 5

chair [tʃeə] Stuhl 9

change [tʃeɪndʒ] umsteigen 6

chap [tʃæp] Kerl 10

charge [tʃɑːdʒ] Kosten 7

check in [tʃek 'ɪn] sich abfertigen lassen 1

cheerio [tʃɪərɪ'əʊ] tschüs 2

cheers [tʃɪəz] Prost 2

cheese [tʃiːz] Käse 12

  Cheddar cheese ['tʃedə tʃiːz] Cheddar-Käse 12

chemical engineer ['kemɪkl endʒɪ'nɪə] Chemotechniker(in) 5

(the) chemist's ['kemɪsts] Apotheke 12

cheque [tʃek] Scheck 8

cheque book ['tʃek bʊk] Scheckbuch, -heft 8

chess [tʃes] Schach 5

chest of drawers ['tʃest əv 'drɔːz] Kommode 9

child, children [tʃaɪld, 'tʃɪldrən] Kind(er) 5

chocolate ['tʃɒkələt] Schokolade 10

  a bar of chocolate ['bɑːr əv 'tʃɒkələt] eine Tafel Schokolade 12

chocolates ['tʃɒkələts] Pralinen 12

  a box of chocolates ein Kasten Konfekt 12

choose [tʃuːz] wählen 10

church [tʃɜːtʃ] Kirche 5

cigar [sɪ'gɑː] Zigarre 10

cigarette [sɪgə'ret] Zigarette 1

cinema ['sɪnəmə] Kino 3

city ['sɪtɪ] Stadt 9

(the) City ['sɪtɪ] Banken- und Geschäftsviertel Londons 6

classes ['klɑːsɪz] Unterricht 7

classical ['klæsɪkl] klassisch 5

clean the house ['kliːn ðə 'haʊs] saubermachen 7

clerk [klɑːk] Angestellte(r) 1; Schalterbeamter 8

clock [klɒk] Uhr 13

  at ten o'clock [əten ə'klɒk] um zehn (Uhr) 3

close [kləʊz] schließen 2

clothes [kləʊðz] Kleidung 10

cloudy ['klaʊdɪ] wolkig, bewölkt 2

club [klʌb] Klub 3

cm = centimetre ['sentɪmiːtə] Zentimeter 10

c/o = care of ['keərəv] per Adresse, bei 7

coach [kəʊtʃ] (Reise-, Flughafen-)Bus 1

coast [kəʊst] Küste 8

code [kəʊd] Vorwahl(nummer) 4

coffee ['kɒfɪ] Kaffee 2

coffee house ['kɒfɪ haʊs] Café 11

coffee table ['kɒfɪ teɪbl] Couchtisch 9

coffin ['kɒfɪn] Sarg 8

cold [kəʊld] kalt 2

colour ['kʌlə] Farbe 4

come [kʌm] kommen 4

  come in [kʌm 'ɪn] hereinkommen 5

  come over [kʌm 'əʊvə] her(über)kommen 12

comedy ['kɒmɪdɪ] Komödie 3

comfortable ['kʌmfətəbl] bequem 9

committee [kə'mɪtɪ] Komitee 8

Commonwealth ['kɒmənwelθ] Staatenbund Großbritanniens mit ehemaligen Kolonien 1

company ['kʌmpənɪ] Gesellschaft 12

compare [kəm'peə] vergleichen 6

complicated ['kɒmplɪkeɪtɪd] kompliziert 4

concert ['kɒnsət] Konzert 3

conference ['kɒnfərəns] Konferenz 8

contest ['kɒntest] Wettkampf 5

conversation [kɒnvə'seɪʃn] Gespräch, Unterhaltung 2

cook [kʊk] Koch, Köchin 1

cooking ['kʊkɪŋ] Kochen 5

corner ['kɔːnə] Ecke 9

corn flakes ['kɔːnfleɪks] Cornflakes 12

correct [kə'rekt] richtig 12

cost [kɒst] kosten 12

could [kʊd] konnte, könnte 3
counter [ˈkaʊntə] Theke 13
country [ˈkʌntrɪ] Land 4
country cottage [ˈkʌntrɪ ˈkɒtɪdʒ] Landhaus 4
couple [ˈkʌpl] Paar 9
course [kɔːs] Kurs 11
crisp [krɪsp] knusprig 12
  crisp bread Knäckebrot 12
crocodile [ˈkrɒkədaɪl] Krokodil 12
crossword [ˈkrɒswɜːd] Kreuzworträtsel 3
crowd [kraʊd] (Menschen-)Menge 12
crown [kraʊn] Krone 2
cultural [ˈkʌltʃərəl] kulturell, Kultur- 11
culture [ˈkʌltʃə] Kultur 5
cup [kʌp] Tasse 2
cupboard [ˈkʌbəd] Schrank 9
cut out [kʌt ˈaʊt] ausschneiden 12

d

dance [dɑːns] tanzen 5
  dinner dance [ˈdɪnə dɑːns] Abendgesellschaft mit Tanz 5
dancing [ˈdɑːnsɪŋ] Tanzen 5
Danish pastry [ˈdeɪnɪʃ ˈpeɪstrɪ] Blätterteiggebäck 12
dark [dɑːk] dunkel 10
date [deɪt] Datum 1
day [deɪ] Tag 2
dead [ded] tot 12
dear [dɪə] liebe(e, s) 7; Liebling 10
  oh dear! [əʊ ˈdɪə] O je! Ach! 13
December [dɪˈsembə] Dezember 11
decide [dɪˈsaɪd] entscheiden 7
departure [dɪˈpɑːtʃə] Abfahrt, Abflug 4
(it) depends [ɪt dɪˈpendz] (es) hängt davon ab, kommt darauf an 7
describe [dɪˈskraɪb] beschreiben 10
description [dɪˈskrɪpʃn] Beschreibung 10
design engineer [dɪˈzaɪn endʒɪˈnɪə] Ingenieur für Formgebung 1
destination [destɪˈneɪʃn] Zielort 4
detail [ˈdiːteɪl] Detail, Einzelheit 8
develop [dɪˈveləp] entwickeln 6
dial [ˈdaɪəl] wählen (Nummer) 4
dialling tone [ˈdaɪəlɪŋ təʊn] Wählton 4
dialogue [ˈdaɪəlɒg] Dialog 3
diary [ˈdaɪərɪ] Tagebuch, Kalender 4
die [daɪ] sterben 9
difficult [ˈdɪfɪkəlt] schwierig 4
digit [ˈdɪdʒɪt] Ziffer 4
dinner [ˈdɪnə] Abendessen 3

have dinner zu Abend essen 3
direkt [dɪˈrekt] direkt 4
direction [dɪˈrekʃn] Anweisung 6
dirty [ˈdɜːtɪ] schmutzig 4
disco [ˈdɪskəʊ] Disko(thek) 3
dislikes [ˈdɪslaɪks] Abneigungen 5
district [ˈdɪstrɪkt] Bezirk 9
  district nurse Bezirkskrankenschwester 7
divide [dɪˈvaɪd] teilen 10
divorced [dɪˈvɔːst] geschieden 6
doctor [ˈdɒktə] Arzt 2
down [daʊn] senkrecht 5
downstairs [daʊnˈsteəz] unten, hinunter 3
dozens of [ˈdʌznz əv] Dutzende von 11
draw [drɔː] zeichnen 9
drawer [ˈdrɔːə] Schub(fach) 11
dress [dres] Kleid 10
drink [drɪŋk] Getränk 2; trinken 5
drive [draɪv] fahren 5

e

each [iːtʃ] jede(r, s) (einzelne) 5
each other [iːtʃ ˈʌðə] sich, einander 10
ear [ɪə] Ohr 12
early [ˈɜːlɪ] früh, zeitig 10
(the) earth [ðɪ ˈɜːθ] (die) Erde 11
  where on earth wo um Himmels willen 11
east [iːst] Osten 5
(the) east coast [ðɪ ˈiːst kəʊst] (die) Ostküste 11
easy [ˈiːzɪ] leicht 3
eat [iːt] essen 7
e.g. = **for example** [fər ɪgˈzɑːmpl] z. B., zum Beispiel 1
egg [eg] Ei 12
eight [eɪt] acht 1
eighteen [eɪˈtiːn] achtzehn 4
eighty [ˈeɪtɪ] achtzig 5
either [ˈaɪðə] auch nicht 6
elephant [ˈelɪfənt] Elefant 12
eleven [ɪˈlevn] elf 2
else [els] noch 12
end [end] Ende, Schluß 2
  in the end [ɪn ðɪ ˈend] am Ende, schließlich 3
engineer [endʒɪˈnɪə] Ingenieur 1
enjoy [ɪnˈdʒɔɪ] genießen 11
enormous [ɪˈnɔːməs] riesig, gewaltig 4
enough [ɪˈnʌf] genug, ausreichend 9
entertainment [entəˈteɪnmənt] Unterhaltung 3

etc. [ɪtˈsetrə] = **and so on** [ənd səʊ ˈɒn] usw., und so weiter 1
evening [ˈiːvnɪŋ] Abend 2
every [ˈevrɪ] jede(r, s) 4
everything [ˈevrɪθɪŋ] alles 3
everywhere [ˈevrɪweə] überall(hin) 9
exactly [ɪgˈzæktlɪ] genau 12
example [ɪgˈzɑːmpl] Beispiel 1
excuse [ɪkˈskjuːz] entschuldigen 1
exercise [ˈeksəsaɪz] Übung 1
expect [ɪkˈspekt] annehmen, vermuten 6
expensive [ɪkˈspensɪv] teuer 3
extra [ˈekstrə] extra, gesondert 12
eye [aɪ] Auge 10

f

fact [fækt] Tatsache 4
  in fact tatsächlich, in der Tat 4
factory [ˈfæktərɪ] Fabrik 4
fair [feə] blond, hell 10
family [ˈfæməlɪ] Familie 3
family name [ˈfæməlɪ neɪm] Familien-, Nachname 1
famous [ˈfeɪməs] berühmt 2
fast [fɑːst] schnell 6
fat [fæt] dick, korpulent 10
father [ˈfɑːðə] Vater 1
favourite [ˈfeɪvərɪt] Lieblings- 2
feature [ˈfiːtʃə] Kennzeichen, Merkmal 10
February [ˈfebrʊərɪ] Februar 11
a few [ə ˈfjuː] einige, ein paar 5
fifteen [fɪfˈtiːn] fünfzehn 4
fifty [ˈfɪftɪ] fünfzig 4
fill in [fɪl ˈɪn] ausfüllen 1
film [fɪlm] Film 1
find [faɪnd] finden, suchen 3
fine [faɪn] fein, schön, gut 2
first [fɜːst] erste(r, s) 4; zuerst 4
first-class [ˈfɜːst klɑːs] erstklassig 3
first name [fɜːst ˈneɪm] Vorname 10
fish [fɪʃ] fischen 5; Fisch 12
  go fishing angeln (gehen) 5
fisherman [ˈfɪʃəmən] Fischer 7
five [faɪv] fünf 1
flat [flæt] Wohnung 4
flight [flaɪt] Flug 1
floor [flɔː] Etage, Stock(werk) 9
  on the first floor im ersten Stock 9
floor show [ˈflɔː ʃəʊ] Nachtklubvorstellung 3
fly [flaɪ] fliegen 8; Fliege 12
following [ˈfɒləʊɪŋ] folgende(r, s) 7

food [fuːd] Essen, Nahrung   3
foot, feet [fʊt, fiːt] Fuß, Füße   12
football [ˈfʊtbɔːl] Fußball   5
footballer [ˈfʊtbɔːlə] Fußballspieler   2
for [fə] für   1
   for example [fər ɪgˈzɑːmpl] zum
    Beispiel   1
foreign [ˈfɒrɪn] ausländisch, fremd   1
foreigner [ˈfɒrɪnə] Ausländer(in),
   Fremde(r)   5
forename [ˈfɔːneim] Vorname   1
forget [fəˈget] vergessen   2
form [fɔːm] Formular   2
forty [ˈfɔːtɪ] vierzig   4
four [fɔː] vier   1
fourteen [fɔːˈtiːn] vierzehn   4
free [friː] frei   7
Friday [ˈfraɪdɪ] Freitag   2
fried [fraɪd] gebraten   12
friend [frend] Freund(in)   2
friendly [ˈfrendlɪ] freundlich   3
from [frəm] von   1
in front of [ɪn ˈfrʌnt əv] vor   13
fruit [fruːt] Früchte, Obst   12
fruit machine [ˈfruːt məʃiːn]
   Spielautomat   13
full [fʊl] voll   1
   we're full wir sind (voll) besetzt   3
full insurance [ˈfʊl ɪnˈʃʊərəns] volle
   Versicherung, Vollkasko   7
fun [fʌn] Spaß   1
funeral [ˈfjuːnərəl] Begräbnis   8
funny [ˈfʌnɪ] seltsam 2; komisch,
   lustig   12
furniture [ˈfɜːnɪtʃə] Möbel   9
further [ˈfɜːðə] weiter(e)   8

g

game [geɪm] Spiel   5
gap [gæp] Lücke   7
garage [ˈgærɑːdʒ] Garage, Werkstatt,
   Tankstelle   6
garden [ˈgɑːdn] Garten   5
gee [dʒiː] Herrje   10
gentleman [ˈdʒentlmən] Gentleman,
   Herr   8
get [get] erhalten, bekommen 3;
   besorgen   7
get to [ˈget tʊ] kommen nach   6
get up [get ˈʌp] aufstehen   5
girl [gɜːl] Mädchen   1
girl friend [ˈgɜːl frend] Freundin   1
give [gɪv] geben   1
give up [gɪv ˈʌp] aufgeben   10

glad [glæd] froh   10
glass [glɑːs] Glas   12
glasses [ˈglɑːsɪz] Spiegel 9; Brille   10
go [gəʊ] gehen, fahren   1
go down [gəʊ ˈdaʊn] sich senken   8
go out [gəʊ ˈaʊt] ausgehen   3
going to [ˈgəʊɪŋ tə] werden   7
God [gɒd] Gott   1
   my God [maɪ ˈgɒd] mein Gott   1
golf [gɒlf] Golf   5
good [gʊd] gut   2
goodbye [gʊdˈbaɪ] Auf Wiedersehn   2
(thank) goodness [ˈθæŋk ˈgʊdnɪs] Gott
   sei Dank   7
got [gɒt] bekam   3
gram [græm] Gramm   1
gray Am. = **grey** [greɪ] grau   10
great [greɪt] großartig, herrlich   10
   it sure is great das ist ja wirklich
    prima   10
green [griːn] grün   9
greeting [ˈgriːtɪŋ] Gruß   2
grey [greɪ] grau   10
group [gruːp] Gruppe   6
guess [ges] glauben   3
guest [gest] Gast   11
guitar [gɪˈtɑː] Gitarre   6

h

had [hæd] hatte   3
hair [heə] Haar(e)   10
ham [hæm] Schinken   12
handbag [ˈhændbæg] Handtasche   4
handy [ˈhændɪ] bequem,
   praktisch   9
happen [ˈhæpən] geschehen,
   passieren   12
harbour [ˈhɑːbə] Hafen   7
hard [hɑːd] hart, schwer   2
has (got) [hæz (ˈgɒt)] hat   1
have [hæv] haben   2
he [hiː] er   1
Head of State [ˈhed əv ˈsteɪt]
   Staatsoberhaupt   6
hear [hɪə] hören   9
hecto [ˈhektəʊ] 100 Gramm   12
height [haɪt] Größe   10
help [help] Hilfe 2; helfen   5
her [hɜː] ihr(e)   4
here's = here is [hɪəz, hɪərˈɪz] hier
   ist   1
hidden [ˈhɪdn] versteckt   3
high [haɪ] hoch   9
hire [haɪə] (ver-)mieten 7; Verleih   7

his [hɪz] sein(e)   2
hitch-hike [ˈhɪtʃhaɪk] per Anhalter
   reisen   8
hold on [ˈhəʊld ˈɒn] (am Apparat)
   bleiben   11
holiday [ˈhɒlədɪ] Feiertag, Ferien,
   Urlaub   5
home [həʊm] Heim   3
   at home [ət ˈhəʊm] zu Hause   3
homeless [ˈhəʊmlɪs] obdachlos   9
(be) homesick [bɪ ˈhəʊmsɪk] an
   Heimweh leiden   7
hope [həʊp] hoffen   11
horrible [ˈhɒrəbl] furchtbar,
   schrecklich   2
hospital [ˈhɒspɪtl] Krankenhaus   11
host [həʊst] Gastgeber   9
hostess [ˈhəʊstɪs] Gastgeberin   9
hot [hɒt] heiß, warm   2
hot water bottle [hɒt ˈwɔːtə ˈbɒtl]
   Wärmflasche   5
hotel [həʊˈtel] Hotel   1
hour [ˈaʊə] Stunde   3
   the hours [ðɪ ˈaʊəz] die Arbeitszeit   3
   four hours [fər ˈaʊəz] stundenlang   7
house [haʊs] Haus   5
housewife [ˈhaʊswaɪf] Hausfrau   1
housing problem [ˈhaʊzɪŋ ˈprɒbləm]
   Wohnungsproblem   9
how [haʊ] wie   1
how much is it? was kostet es?   7
how to say it wie man etwas sagt   1
hullo [həˈləʊ] hallo, guten Tag   1
hundred [ˈhʌndrəd] hundert   1
husband [ˈhʌzbənd] (Ehe-)Mann   1

i

I [aɪ] ich   1
ice-cream [aɪsˈkriːm] (Speise-)Eis   12
I'd = I would [aɪd, aɪ ˈwʊd] ich
   würde   11
idea [aɪˈdɪə] Idee   3
idiomatic [ɪdɪəˈmætɪk] idiomatisch   1
if [ɪf] wenn 1; ob   11
I'm = I am [aɪm, aɪ ˈæm] ich bin   1
immigration act [ɪmɪˈgreɪʃn ækt]
   Einwanderungsgesetz   1
in [ɪn] in   1
include [ɪnˈkluːd] einschließen   7
information [ɪnfəˈmeɪʃn]
   Information(en), Hinweis(e)   1
instant [ˈɪnstənt] sofort löslich   12
instant coffee [ˈɪnstənt ˈkɒfɪ]
   Pulverkaffee   12

instead [ɪnˈsted] anstatt 6
insurance [ɪnˈʃʊərəns] Versicherung 7
intelligent [ɪnˈtelɪdʒənt] intelligent 10
interest [ˈɪntrɪst] Interesse 5
interested [ˈɪntrɪstɪd] interessiert 3
interesting [ˈɪntrɪstɪŋ] interessant 2
international [ɪntəˈnæʃənl]
   international 4
interview [ˈɪntəvjuː] Interview 5
into [ˈɪntʊ] hinein 1
introduce [ɪntrəˈdjuːs] vorstellen 1
invitation [ɪnvɪˈteɪʃn] Einladung 11
invite [ɪnˈvaɪt] einladen 11
is [ɪz] ist 1
it [ɪt] es 1
it's = **it is** [ɪts, ɪt ˈɪz] es ist 1
it's (= **it has**) **got** [ɪts, ɪt həz ˈgɒt] es
   hat 3
its [ɪts] sein(e) 4

j

jacket [ˈdʒækɪt] Jacke, Jackett 10
January [ˈdʒænjʊərɪ] Januar 11
jazz [dʒæz] Jazz 3
jeans [dʒiːnz] Jeans 10
job [dʒɒb] Beruf 1
joke [dʒəʊk] scherzen 12; Scherz 12
journalist [ˈdʒɜːnəlɪst] Journalist(in) 10
judo [ˈdʒuːdəʊ] Judo 5
juice [dʒuːs] Saft 12
July [dʒʊˈlaɪ] Juli 11
June [dʒuːn] Juni 11
just [dʒʌst] nur 2; gerade 11

k

kangaroo [kæŋgəˈruː] Känguruh 6
kilo [ˈkiːləʊ] Kilo 12
kilometre [ˈkɪləʊmiːtə] Kilometer 6
kind [kaɪnd] freundlich 11
kind of [ˈkaɪnd əv] (eine) Art von 6
king [kɪŋ] König 11
kitchen [ˈkɪtʃɪn] Küche 9
know [nəʊ] wissen 4; kennen 6
   you know du weißt schon 4
KLM [ˈkeɪ el ˈem] 1
koala bear [kəʊˈɑːlə beə] Koalabär 6

l

lady [ˈleɪdɪ] Dame 3
lake [leɪk] See 9
lamp [læmp] Lampe 9

landing card [ˈlændɪŋ kɑːd]
   Einreisekarte 1
landlord [ˈlændlɔːd] (Gast-)Wirt 2
language [ˈlæŋgwɪdʒ] Sprache 10
large [lɑːdʒ] groß 5
lasagne [ləˈsanjə] überbackene Nudeln
   mit Fleischsauce 12
last [lɑːst] letzte(r,s) 7
   at last [ət ˈlɑːst] zuletzt, schließlich 11
late [leɪt] (zu) spät 1
latest [ˈleɪtɪst] letzte(r,s),
   neueste(r, s) 7
leave [liːv] verlassen 1
left [left] links 9
   on the left [ɒn ðə ˈleft] auf der linken
   Seite 2
lessons [ˈlesnz] Unterricht 7
let [let] vermieten 9
let's [lets] laß uns, wollen wir 3
   let's see [lets ˈsiː] laß mal sehen 11
letter [ˈletə] Brief 7
   block letters [ˈblɒk letəz]
   Druckbuchstaben 1
librarian [laɪˈbreərɪən]
   Bibliothekar(in) 7
library [ˈlaɪbrərɪ] Bücherei,
   Bibliothek 7
life [laɪf] (das) Leben 4
(give a) lift [lɪft] im Auto
   mitnehmen 13
light [laɪt] Licht, Feuer 8
light green [laɪt ˈgriːn] hellgrün 9
like [laɪk] wie 2; gern haben, mögen 2
   what's he like? wie ist er? 9
   like this so, in dieser Art 1
likes [laɪks] Vorlieben 5
list [lɪst] Liste 12
listen [ˈlɪsn] (zu-)hören 4
   listen to zuhören 5
litre [ˈliːtə] Liter 1
little [ˈlɪtl] klein 4
lively [ˈlaɪvlɪ] lebhaft 10
local paper [ˈləʊkl ˈpeɪpə]
   Lokalzeitung 12
lonely [ˈləʊnlɪ] einsam 10
long [lɒŋ] lang 3
look [lʊk] sehen, blicken 1
   look after [lʊk ˈɑːftə] sich kümmern
   um 5
   look for [ˈlʊk fə] suchen 10
   look up [lʊk ˈʌp] aufblicken 10
a lot [ə ˈlɒt] viel(e), eine Menge 5
a lot of [ə ˈlɒt əv] viel(e), eine
   Menge 3

lots of [ˈlɒts əv] viel(e), eine Menge 2
loud [laʊd] laut 12
love [lʌv] lieben 11
   I'd love to [aɪd ˈlʌv tʊ] ich würde (es)
   sehr gern 11
Love, [lʌv] Herzlich(e Grüße), 7
lovely [ˈlʌvlɪ] wunderbar 2
lunch [lʌntʃ] Mittagessen 4
luxury [ˈlʌkʃərɪ] Luxus 7

m

madam [ˈmædəm] gnädige Frau 7
make [meɪk] machen, bilden 1
male [meɪl] männlich 1
man, men [mæn, men] Mann, Männer,
   Herr(en) 1
manager [ˈmænɪdʒə] Chef, Direktor 10
   assistant manager Chefassistent 1
many [ˈmenɪ] viel(e) 5
map [mæp] (Land-)Karte 8
March [mɑːtʃ] März 11
market [ˈmɑːkɪt] Markt 11
married [ˈmærɪd] verheiratet 2
match [mætʃ] (Fußball-)Spiel 2;
   Streichholz 12
May [meɪ] Mai 11
me [miː] mir, mich 1
   Monique and me Monique und
   ich 11
mean [miːn] meinen, bedeuten 2
mechanic [mɪˈkænɪk] Mechaniker,
   Monteur 9
medium [ˈmiːdjəm] mittel, rosa 12
meet [miːt] treffen 1
meeting [ˈmiːtɪŋ] Treffen 8
menu [ˈmenjuː] Speisekarte 12
mermaid [ˈmɜːmeɪd] Seejungfrau 12
method [ˈmeθəd] Methode, Art und
   Weise 13
midnight [ˈmɪdnaɪt] Mitternacht 7
   by midnight (spätestens) bis
   Mitternacht 7
mile [maɪl] Meile (= 1,6 km) 7
mileage [ˈmaɪlɪdʒ] Kilometerstand,
   -zahl 7
milk [mɪlk] Milch 2
million [ˈmɪljən] Million 5
mind [maɪnd] beachten 12
mine [maɪn] mein(e) 10
minute [ˈmɪnɪt] Minute 1
Miss [mɪs] Fräulein 1
missing [ˈmɪsɪŋ] fehlende(r, s),
   vermißt 3
   be missing vermißt werden 10

model ['mɒdl] Modell   7
modern ['mɒdən] modern   9
Monday ['mʌndɪ] Montag   1
money ['mʌnɪ] Geld   3
  make money Geld verdienen   3
month [mʌnθ] Monat   4
more [mɔ:] mehr   1
  more . . . than [ðən] mehr . . . als   6
morning ['mɔ:nɪŋ] Morgen,
  Vormittag   1
most [məʊst] meist, am meisten   2, 3
  most of them die meisten von
  ihnen   2
mother ['mʌðə] Mutter   1
moustache [mə'stɑ:ʃ] Schnurrbart   10
mouth [maʊθ] Mund   10
Mr ['mɪstə] Herr (vor Namen)   1
Mrs ['mɪsɪz] Frau (vor Namen)   1
much [mʌtʃ] viel   5
museum [mju:'zɪəm] Museum   5
music ['mju:zɪk]   3
musical ['mju:zɪkl] Musical   3
must [mʌst] müssen   1
my [maɪ] mein(e)   1

n

name [neɪm] Name   1
nasty ['nɑ:stɪ] unangenehm,
  widerlich   2
nationality [næʃə'nælətɪ] Nationalität,
  Staatsangehörigkeit   1
near [nɪə] nahe, in der Nähe von   9
nearly ['nɪəlɪ] beinahe, fast   6
need [ni:d] brauchen   1
never ['nevə] niemals   1
never mind ['nevə 'maɪnd] (das) macht
  nichts   12
new [nju:] neu   2
next [nekst] nächste(r, s)   7
nice [naɪs] schön   2
night [naɪt] Nacht, Abend   3
nine [naɪn] neun   1
nineteen [naɪn'ti:n] neunzehn   4
ninety ['naɪntɪ] neunzig   5
no [nəʊ] nein   1
  that's no good das geht nicht   8
noisy ['nɔɪzɪ] laut   3
nor do I ['nɔ: dʊ 'aɪ] ich auch nicht   5
north [nɔ:θ] Norden   5
Northern ['nɔ:ðən] nördlich   6
not [nɒt] nicht   1
  not . . . any kein   12
note [nəʊt] beachten 4; (Bank-)Note,
  (Geld-)Schein   8

nothing ['nʌθɪŋ] nichts   4
November [nəʊ'vembə]
  November   11
now [naʊ] nun, jetzt   1
nowadays ['naʊədeɪz] heutzutage   4
number ['nʌmbə] Nummer, Zahl   2
nurse [nɜ:s] Krankenschwester,
  -pfleger(in)   1
nut [nʌt] Nuß   12

o

occupation [ɒkjʊ'peɪʃn] Beruf   1
o'clock [ə'klɒk] Uhr   3
October [ɒk'təʊbə] Oktober   11
of [əv] von   1
of course [əf 'kɔ:s] natürlich   4
offer ['ɒfə] anbieten   12
office ['ɒfɪs] Büro   1
official [ə'fɪʃl] amtlich   1
  for official use [fər ə'fɪʃl 'ju:s] für
  amtliche Vermerke   1
oh [əʊ] o, ach   1
okay [əʊ'keɪ] gut, in Ordnung   7
old [əʊld] alt   1
old-fashioned [əʊld'fæʃnd] altmodisch,
  unmodern   9
omit [ə'mɪt] aus-, weglassen   4
one [wʌn] ein(s, e)   1
only ['əʊnlɪ] nur   6
open ['əʊpən] offen, öffnen   2
opinion [ə'pɪnjən] Meinung, Ansicht   1
opposite ['ɒpəzɪt] gegenüber   9
or [ɔ:] oder   1
orange ['ɒrɪndʒ] Apfelsine,
  Orange   12
orchestra ['ɔ:kɪstrə] Orchester   3
order ['ɔ:də] Reihenfolge 7;
  bestellen   10
ordinary ['ɔ:dnrɪ] gewöhnlich   2
organise ['ɔ:gənaɪz] organisieren   6
other ['ʌðə] andere(r, s)   1
ounce [aʊns] Unze (= 28 g)   1
our ['aʊə] unser(e)   1
out [aʊt] aus   3
outside [aʊt'saɪd] außerhalb   11
over ['əʊvə] über   2
over there [əʊvə 'ðeə] dort, da
  drüben   4
overcrowded [əʊvə'kraʊdɪd]
  überfüllt   9
overcrowding [əʊvə'kraʊdɪŋ]
  Überbevölkerung   9
owe [əʊ] schulden, schuldig sein   8
own [əʊn] eigen(e)   10

p

p = pence [pi:, pens] Pence (englische
  Währung)   12
packet ['pækɪt] Päckchen   12
page [peɪdʒ] Seite   3
pair [peə] Paar   1
  a pair of shoes [ə 'peər ev 'ʃu:z] ein
  Paar Schuhe   10
palace ['pælɪs] Palast, Schloß   11
paper shop ['peɪpə ʃɒp]
  Zeitungsladen   12
park [pɑ:k] Park   9
partner ['pɑ:tnə] Partner   5
part time ['pɑ:t taɪm] halbtags   5
party ['pɑ:tɪ] Party, Gesellschaft   2
  have a party eine Party geben   6
passenger ['pæsɪndʒə] Passagier   1
passport ['pɑ:spɔ:t] Paß   1
pay [peɪ] Bezahlung, Verdienst   3
pen [pen] Füller, Kugelschreiber   8
pence [pens], **penny** ['penɪ] Pence
  (englische Währung)   12
pensioner ['penʃənə] Pensionär(in),
  Rentner(in)   6
people ['pi:pl] Leute, Menschen   1
per [pə] pro   12
perfect ['pɜ:fɪkt] perfekt, richtig   8
perhaps [pə'hæps] vielleicht   6
person ['pɜ:sn] Person   1
personal ['pɜ:snl] persönlich   5
phone [fəʊn] Telefon 4; anrufen   4
phone call ['fəʊn kɔ:l]
  (Telefon-)Anruf   4
photo ['fəʊtəʊ] Photo(graphie)   1
phrase [freɪz] Wendung, Ausdruck   1
piano [pɪ'ænəʊ] Klavier   6
pick up [pɪk 'ʌp] (auf-)nehmen 8;
  abholen   13
picnic ['pɪknɪk] Picknick   7
picture ['pɪktʃə] Bild   1
piece of furniture [pi:s əv 'fɜ:nɪtʃə]
  Möbelstück   9
pilot ['paɪlət] Pilot   1
place [pleɪs] Ort   2
place of birth ['pleɪs əv 'bɜ:θ]
  Geburtsort   1
plan [plæn] Plan 3; planen   7
plane [pleɪn] Flugzeug   5
planning ['plænɪŋ] Planen   7
plant [plɑ:nt] Pflanze   13
plate [pleɪt] Teller, Platte   12
play [pleɪ] (Schau-)Spiel, Stück 3;
  spielen   5
please [pli:z] bitte   2

plumber ['plʌmə] Klempner, Installateur 8

p.m. [pi:'em] nachmittags 3

pocket ['pɒkɪt] Tasche 11

poker ['pəʊkə] Poker 13

policeman [pə'li:smən] Polizist 1

police station [pə'li:s steɪʃn] Polizeirevier, -wache 9

polite [pə'laɪt] höflich 5

pop concert ['pɒp 'kɒnsət] Schlagerkonzert 3

popular ['pɒpjʊlə] populär, beliebt 3

population [pɒpjʊ'leɪʃn] Bevölkerung, Einwohner(zahl) 6

pork chop ['pɔ:k tʃɒp] Schweinekotelett 12

portion ['pɔ:ʃn] Portion 12

postcard ['pəʊstkɑ:d] Postkarte 7

post office ['pəʊst ɒfɪs] Post(amt) 2

potato(es) [pə'teɪtəʊ(z)] Kartoffel(n) 12

pound (£) [paʊnd] Pfund (englische Währung) 4

powerful ['paʊəfʊl] stark, mächtig 6

practise ['præktɪs] üben 1

prefer [prɪ'fɜ:] bevorzugen, vorziehen 5

preposition [prepə'zɪʃn] Präposition 9

price [praɪs] Preis 3

prince [prɪns] Prinz 13

princess ['prɪnses] Prinzessin 13

probably ['prɒbəblɪ] wahrscheinlich 9

problem ['prɒbləm] Problem 1

programme ['prəʊgræm] Programm 10

proper ['prɒpə] richtig, ordentlich 9

pub [pʌb] Pub 2

put [pʊt] setzen, stellen, legen 1

put right [pʊt 'raɪt] berichtigen, richtigstellen 6

puzzle ['pʌzl] Rätsel 3

q

quarter ['kwɔ:tə] viertel 8

queen [kwi:n] Königin 6

question ['kwestʃn] Frage 1

quiet ['kwaɪət] ruhig, still 9

quite [kwaɪt] ganz 9

r

radiator ['reɪdɪeɪtə] Heizkörper 13

railway station ['reɪlweɪ steɪʃn] Bahnhof 7

rain [reɪn] regnen 8

rare [reə] blutig 12

rate [reɪt] Preis 7

rather ['rɑ:ðə] ziemlich 6

read [ri:d] lesen 1

real [rɪəl] wirklich, richtig 3

really ['rɪəlɪ] wirklich, tatsächlich 3; in der Tat 9

reasonable ['ri:znəbl] vernünftig, angemessen 3

reception [rɪ'sepʃn] Empfang 2

recognise ['rekəgnaɪz] anerkennen 6

red [red] rot 4

remember [rɪ'membə] (sich) erinnern, einprägen 12

rent [rent] Miete, mieten 9

reply [rɪ'plaɪ] antworten 10

report [rɪ'pɔ:t] berichten 10

republic [rɪ'pʌblɪk] Republik 6

restaurant ['restərɒnt] Restaurant 2

result [rɪ'zʌlt] Resultat 10

retired [rɪ'taɪəd] pensioniert, im Ruhestand 11

return [rɪ'tɜ:n] (hin und) zurück 7; zurückbringen 7

reverse [rɪ'vɜ:s] umkehren, umdrehen 7

ride [raɪd] reiten 5

right [raɪt] richtig 1; rechts 9
  on the right auf der rechten Seite 9
  right over genau gegenüber 6

ring [rɪŋ] klingeln, läuten 4

roast [rəʊst] braten, rösten 12

roast beef ['rəʊst bi:f] Rinderbraten 12

rock music ['rɒk mju:zɪk] Rockmusik 5

rock'n'roll ['rɒkn'rəʊl] Rock and Roll 3

role play ['rəʊlpleɪ] Rollenspiel 1

room [ru:m] Zimmer 2

rose [rəʊz] Rose 2

round [raʊnd] durch 8

routing number ['ru:tɪŋ nʌmbə] Ortsnetzkennzahl 4

(the) Royal Pavilion [ðə 'rɔɪəl pə'vɪljən] der Königliche Pavillon 11

s

sail [seɪl] segeln 5

sailor ['seɪlə] Seemann, Matrose 11

salad ['sæləd] Salat 12

sales conference ['seɪlz kɒnfərəns] Verkaufsbesprechung 8

salesman ['seɪlzmən] Verkäufer 8

same [seɪm] selbe 9
  all the same trotz(alle)dem 9; alle gleich 10

sandwich ['sænwɪdʒ] belegtes (Weiß-)Brot 12

SAS = Scandinavian Airlines System ['es eɪ 'es, skændɪ'neɪvjən 'eəlaɪnz 'sɪstəm] 1

Saturday ['sætədɪ] Sonnabend, Samstag 2

say [seɪ] sagen 1

says [sez] sagt 3

school [sku:l] Schule 11

school meeting ['sku:l mi:tɪŋ] Elternabend 11

script girl ['skrɪpt gɜ:l] Scriptgirl 10

sea [si:] See, Meer 6
  by sea [baɪ 'si:] mit dem Schiff 6

seaside ['si:saɪd] Küste 11

seaside town ['si:saɪd taʊn] Seebad 11

second ['sekənd] Sekunde 4; zweite(r, s) 9

secretary ['sekrətrɪ] Sekretär(in) 1

see [si:] sehen 1; besuchen 4; verstehen 5
  see you wir sehen uns 2

send [send] senden, schicken 7

sentence ['sentəns] Satz 1

September [səp'tembə] September 11

serious ['sɪərɪəs] ernst(haft) 3

service ['sɜ:vɪs] Dienst(leistung), Bedienung 8

seven ['sevn] sieben 4

seventeen [sevn'ti:n] siebzehn 4

seventy ['sevntɪ] siebzig 5

several ['sevrəl] mehrere 11

sex [seks] Geschlecht 1

shall [ʃæl] sollen 1, 3
  Shall we go, then? Wollen wir dann gehen? 1

shampoo [ʃæm'pu:] Haarwaschmittel 12

she [ʃi:] sie 1

sherry ['ʃerɪ] Sherry 12

shirt [ʃɜ:t] Hemd 10

shoe [ʃu:] Schuh 10

shop [ʃɒp] Laden, Geschäft 1
  go to the shops einkaufen gehen 12

shop assistant ['ʃɒp ə'sɪstənt] Verkäufer(in) 1

shopkeeper ['ʃɒpki:pə] Ladeninhaber 4

shopping ['ʃɒpɪŋ] Einkaufen 7; Einkauf 12

go shopping, do the shopping einkaufen (gehen) 5, 7

shopping centre ['ʃɒpɪŋ sentə] Einkaufszentrum 9

shopping list ['ʃɒpɪŋ lɪst] Einkaufsliste, -zettel 12

short [ʃɔːt] kurz 3; untersetzt, klein 10

should [ʃʊd] sollte 4

I should think ich meine 10

shower ['ʃaʊə] Dusche 9

shrimp [ʃrɪmp] Garnele, Krabbe 12

side [saɪd] Seite 6

sightseeing tour ['saɪtsiːɪŋ tʊə] Besichtigungsfahrt 8

go sightseeing Sehenswürdigkeiten besichtigen 5

signature ['sɪgnətʃə] Unterschrift 1

silly ['sɪlɪ] albern 6

single ['sɪŋgl] alleinstehend, unverheiratet 6

sir [sɜː] mein Herr 10

sit [sɪt] sitzen 9

sit down [sɪt 'daʊn] sich setzen 5

situation [sɪtjʊ'eiʃn] Situation 9

six [sɪks] sechs 1

sixteen [sɪks'tiːn] sechzehn 4

sixty ['sɪkstɪ] sechzig 5

skate [skeɪt] Schlittschuh laufen 5

skiing ['skiːɪŋ] Schifahren 5

skirt [skɜːt] Rock 10

slim [slɪm] schlank 10

slow [sləʊ] langsam 6

slum [slʌm] Elendsviertel 9

small [smɔːl] klein 3

smart [smɑːt] fesch, schick 10

smile [smaɪl] Lächeln 10

smoke [sməʊk] rauchen 5

so [səʊ] so 3

so that [səʊ ðət] so daß 1

I don't think so ich glaube nicht 3

so do I ['səʊ dʊ 'aɪ] ich auch 5

soap [səʊp] Seife 12

a bar of soap [ə 'bɑːr əv 'səʊp] ein Stück Seife 12

socks [sɒks] Socken 11

sofa ['səʊfə] Sofa 9

some [sʌm] einige 2

someone ['sʌmwʌn] jemand 1

something ['sʌmθɪŋ] etwas 6

sometimes ['sʌmtaɪmz] manchmal 9

song [sɒŋ] Lied 5

sorry ['sɒrɪ] Verzeihung, Entschuldigung 1

sort [sɔːt] Sorte, Art 6

a sort of [ə 'sɔːt əv] eine Art (von) 9

soup [suːp] Suppe 12

south [saʊθ] Süden 5

south of ['saʊθ əv] südlich von 11

(the) South Coast [ðə 'saʊθ kəʊst] die Südküste 8

spare time ['speə taɪm] Freizeit 5

speak [spiːk] sprechen 5

special ['speʃl] besonder(e) 4

spend [spend] verbringen 5

spider ['spaɪdə] Spinne 12

spirits ['spɪrɪts] Alkohol, Spirituosen 1

sport [spɔːt] Sport 5

sports car ['spɔːts kɑː] Sportwagen 7

spring [sprɪŋ] Frühling 11

stamp [stæmp] (Brief-)Marke 12

stand [stænd] stehen 12

star [stɑː] Stern, Star 1

start [stɑːt] beginnen, anfangen 8

state [steɪt] Staat 6

station ['steɪʃn] Bahnhof 2

statistics [stə'tɪstɪks] Statistik 5

stay [steɪ] bleiben 3

steak [steɪk] Steak, Filet 12

still [stɪl] noch 3; doch, trotzdem 9

stop [stɒp] anhalten 6; aufhören 7

bus stop ['bʌs stɒp] Bushaltestelle 2

story ['stɔːrɪ] Geschichte 12

strange [streɪndʒ] seltsam, fremd(artig) 6

street [striːt] Straße 2

strike [straɪk] Streik 5

be on strike streiken 5

strip club ['strɪp klʌb] Nachtklub mit Striptease 3

strong [strɒŋ] stark 5

student ['stjuːdnt] Student(in) 1

studio ['stjuːdɪəʊ] Studio 3

study ['stʌdɪ] studieren 1

subject ['sʌbdʒɪkt] Subjekt 6

subscriber [səb'skraɪbə] Teilnehmer 4

sugar ['ʃʊgə] Zucker 5

suggest [sə'dʒest] vorschlagen 3

suggestion [sə'dʒestʃn] Vorschlag 3

suit [suːt] Anzug 10

summer ['sʌmə] Sommer 6

Sunday ['sʌndɪ] Sonntag 2

sunny ['sʌnɪ] sonnig 2

supermarket ['suːpəmɑːkɪt] Supermarkt 12

sure [ʃʊə] sicher, gewiß 6

surname ['sɜːneɪm] Nach-, Familienname 1

surprised [sə'praɪzd] überrascht 4

sweater ['swetə] Pullover 10

sweet [swiːt] Nachspeise 12

swim [swɪm] schwimmen 12

swimming ['swɪmɪŋ] Schwimmen 5

symphony ['sɪmfənɪ] Sinfonie 3

t

table ['teɪbl] Tisch 9

tail [teɪl] Schwanz 12

take [teɪk] nehmen 2; dauern 6

take to bringen zu, nach, in 2

talk [tɔːk] sprechen 5

tall [tɔːl] groß 10

tax-free ['tæks friː] zollfrei 1

taxi driver ['tæksɪ draɪvə] Taxifahrer 1

taxi rank ['tæksɪ ræŋk] Taxistand 7

tea [tiː] Tee 5

tea shop ['ti ʃɒp] Teestube 12

teach [tiːtʃ] lehren 7

teacher ['tiːtʃə] Lehrer(in) 1

technical college ['teknɪkl 'kɒlɪdʒ] technische Fachhochschule 11

telephone ['telɪfəʊn] Telefon 1

television ['telɪvɪʒn] Fernsehen, Fernseher 3

watch television [wɒtʃ 'telɪvɪʒn] fernsehen 3

tell [tel] sagen, erzählen 4

tell the time die Uhrzeit sagen 8

ten [ten] zehn 1

tennis ['tenɪs] Tennis 5

terminal ['tɜːmɪnl] Abfertigungshalle (auf Flughafen) 1; Haltestelle (für Flughafenbus) 1

terrace ['terəs] Terrasse, Panoramaweg 7

terribly ['terəblɪ] fürchterlich 12

text [tekst] 1

than [ðən] als 1

thank you ['θæŋk jʊ] danke 1

thanks [θæŋks] danke 2

that [ðæt] das 1; jene 3; [ðət] daß 3

that's all right ['ðæts ɔːl raɪt] das ist schon in Ordnung 1

that's right ['ðæts raɪt] das stimmt 1

the [ðə, vor Vokalen ðɪ] der, die das 1

theatre ['θɪətə] Theater 3

their [ðeə] ihr(e) 1

them [ðem] ihnen, sie 1

then [ðen] dann 1

there [ðeə] dort 1

there are [ðeər ɑː, ðərə] es gibt 1

these [ðiːz] diese 1

they [ðeɪ] sie   1
thing [θɪŋ] Ding, Sache   3
think [θɪŋk] denken, glauben   1
third [θɜːd] dritte(r, s)   6
thirteen [θɜːˈtiːn] dreizehn   4
thirty [ˈθɜːtɪ] dreißig   4
this [ðɪs] dies(e, er, es)   1
those [ðəʊz] jene   4
thousand [ˈθaʊznd] tausend   2
three [θriː] drei   1
thriller [ˈθrɪlə] Reißer, spannender
   Film   5
Thursday [ˈθɜːzdɪ] Donnerstag   2
ticket [ˈtɪkɪt] (Fahr-, Theater-,
   Eintritts-)Karte   4
tie [taɪ] Binder, Schlips   10
tiger [ˈtaɪgə] Tiger   12
time [taɪm] Zeit 2; Mal   10
   what's the time? wie spät ist es?   4
time-table [ˈtaɪmteɪbl] Fahrplan   8
to [tʊ, tə] zu, nach, bis   1
toast [təʊst] Toast   12
tobacco [təˈbækəʊ] Tabak   1
today [təˈdeɪ] heute   2
together [təˈgeðə] zusammen   1
toilet [ˈtɔɪlɪt] Toilette, WC   9
tomato(es) [təˈmɑːtəʊ(z)]
   Tomate(n)   12
tomorrow [təˈmɒrəʊ] morgen   3
tonight [təˈnaɪt] heute abend, nacht   3
too [tuː] auch   3
top [tɒp] oberste(r, s)   11
   the top one [ðə ˈtɒp wʌn] der, die,
   das oberste   11
tour [tʊə] (Rund-)Reise 8; bereisen   8
tours manager [ˈtʊəz mænɪdʒə]
   Reiseleiter(in)   10
tourist [ˈtʊərɪst] Tourist(in),
   Reisende(r)   2
town [taʊn] Stadt   3
traditional [trəˈdɪʃənl] traditionell   3
traffic warden [ˈtræfɪk wɔːdn]
   Verkehrswächter(in)   1
train [treɪn] Zug   5
translate [trænsˈleɪt] übersetzen   1
transport [ˈtrænspɔːt] Transport,
   Verkehr   7
travel [ˈtrævl] reisen, fahren   1
travel agents [ˈtrævl eɪdʒənts]
   Reisebüro   9
tray [treɪ] Tablett   13
trip [trɪp] (Kurz-)Reise   7
trouble [ˈtrʌbl] Sorge, Kummer,
   Verdruß   3
trousers [ˈtraʊzəz] Hose   10

try [traɪ] versuchen   1
Tuesday [ˈtjuːzdɪ] Dienstag   2
turn round [tɜːn ˈraʊnd] (sich)
   umdrehen   10
twelve [twelv] zwölf   2
twenty [ˈtwentɪ] zwanzig   4
two [tuː] zwei   1
type [taɪp] Typ   10
typical [ˈtɪpɪkl] typisch   3
typist [ˈtaɪpɪst] Typistin,
   Maschineschreiber(in)   1

u

under [ˈʌndə] unter   1
Underground [ˈʌndəgraʊnd] U-Bahn   6
understand [ʌndəˈstænd]
   verstehen   10
(the) United Kingdom [ðə juːˈnaɪtɪd
   ˈkɪŋdəm] das Vereinigte Königreich
   (England, Schottland, Wales,
   Nordirland)   1
(the) United States [ðə juːˈnaɪtɪd ˈsteɪts]
   die Vereinigten Staaten (von
   Amerika)   6
university [juːnɪˈvɜːsətɪ] Universität   11
upstairs [ʌpˈsteəz] oben, im ersten
   Stock   9
use [juːs] Gebrauch 1; [juːz]
   gebrauchen   1
usually [ˈjuːʒʊəlɪ] gewöhnlich   6

v

very [ˈverɪ] sehr   2
vice versa [vaɪsɪ ˈvɜːsə] umgekehrt   6
visit [ˈvɪzɪt] besuchen 5; Besuch   6
visitor [ˈvɪzɪtə] Besucher(in), Gast   6

w

wait [weɪt] warten   4
waiter [ˈweɪtə] Kellner   1
waitress [ˈweɪtrɪs] Kellnerin   12
wake up [weɪk ˈʌp] aufwecken   4
walk [wɔːk] zu Fuß gehen   7
   go for walks [ˈgəʊ fə ˈwɔːks]
   spazierengehen   5
wall [wɔːl] Wand   9
wallet [ˈwɒlɪt] Brieftasche   4
want (to) [ˈwɒnt (tʊ)] wollen,
   wünschen   1
warm [wɔːm] warm   2

was [wɒz] war   4
   wasn't = was not [ˈwɒznt, wɒz ˈnɒt]
   war nicht   4
watch [wɒtʃ] beobachten   3;
   (Armband-)Uhr   4
   watch television fernsehen   3
wave [weɪv] winken   12
way [weɪ] Art, Weise 7; Weg   9
we [wiː] wir   1
weather [ˈweðə] Wetter   2
Wednesday [ˈwenzdɪ] Mittwoch   2
week [wiːk] Woche   4
weekend [wiːkˈend] Wochenende   4
well [wel] nun 2; gut   6
well-done [welˈdʌn] (gut)
   durchgebraten   12
(the) West Country [ðə ˈwest ˈkʌntrɪ]
   Westengland   8
the West End [ðə ˈwest ˈend]
   (vornehme) Gegend Londons   6
wet [wet] naß   2
what [wɒt] was   1
what about [wɒt əˈbaʊt] wie wäre es
   mit   3
what a pity [ˈwɒt ə ˈpɪtɪ] wie
   schade   11
what's on [wɒts ˈɒn] was ist los?   1
when [wen] wann, wenn 4; als   12
where [weə] wo(hin)   2
where to? [weə ˈtuː] wohin?   8
which [wɪtʃ] welche(r, s)   6
whisky [ˈwɪskɪ] Whisky   1
white [waɪt] weiß   4
who [huː] wer 2; der, die, das   3
why [waɪ] warum   1
wife [waɪf] (Ehe-)Frau   1
will [wɪl] werden   1
window [ˈwɪndəʊ] Fenster   9
windy [ˈwɪndɪ] windig   2
wine [waɪn] Wein   1
winter [ˈwɪntə] Winter   6
wish [wɪʃ] wünschen   7
   best wishes [best ˈwɪʃɪz] mit den
   besten Grüßen   7
with [wɪð] mit   1
without [wɪˈðaʊt] ohne   5
woman, women [ˈwʊmən, ˈwɪmɪn]
   Frau(en)   1
wonderful [ˈwʌndəfʊl] wunderbar   2
word [wɜːd] Wort   1
work [wɜːk] arbeiten 1; Arbeit   1
worker [ˈwɜːkə] Arbeiter(in)   4
world [wɜːld] Welt   4
worried [ˈwʌrɪd] bekümmert   12
worry [ˈwʌrɪ] sich Sorgen machen   12

would [wʊd] würde(n) 3
write [raɪt] schreiben 1
write down [raɪt 'daʊn]
  aufschreiben 5
write out [raɪt 'aʊt] ausschreiben 8
writer ['raɪtə] Schriftsteller(in) 6

wrong [rɒŋ] falsch 2

y

year [jɜ:] Jahr 5
yellow ['jeləʊ] gelb 10
yes [jes] ja 1

you [ju:] du, ihr, Sie 1
young [jʌŋ] jung 3
your [jɔ:] dein(e), euer(e), Ihr(e) 1
yours [jɔ:z] deine(r, s) 13
yourself [jɔ:'self] dich, euch, Sie
  selbst 1

All Right 1   All Right 2

A Refresher Course

Lehrbuch (176 Seiten)
Klettnummer 5028

Rollenspielkarten (118 Karten)
Klettnummer 50284

2 Compact-Cassetten
(mit allen Dialogen, Strukturübungen und
Texten)
Klettnummer 50287

Lehrerband
mit ausführlichen Erläuterungen der
methodisch-didaktischen Konzeption
sowie praktischen Hinweisen für die
Unterrichtsgestaltung
Klettnummer 50283

Lehrbuch (180 Seiten)
Klettnummer 5029

Rollenspielkarten (104 Karten)
Klettnummer 50294

2 Compact-Cassetten
(mit allen Dialogen, Strukturübungen
und Texten)
Klettnummer 50297

Lehrerband
mit ausführlichen Erläuterungen der
methodisch-didaktischen Konzeption
sowie praktischen Hinweisen für die
Unterrichtsgestaltung
Klettnummer 50293

1 The Houses of Parliament
2 Westminster Abbey
3 Scotland Yard
4 Whitehall lined with Government Offices
5 Downing Street
6 London County Hall
7 Westminster Bridge
8 Charing Cross Bridge
9 Waterloo Bridge

The West End:
Regent Street,
a major shopping
street.

The Strand (by Charing Cross Station).

The Lord Mayor in his golden coach, passes the Law Courts in the Lord Mayor's Show.

173

A car driving onto the hovercraft-ferry "The Princess Anne" at Dover.

Victoria Station.

Rugby League Football – a rough game in which broken bones are common.

Village Cricket – The ball has just been bowled and the batsman will try to hit it.

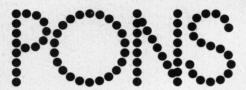

PONS Reisewörterbücher

Sprachführer und Wörterbuch zugleich. Auf über 200 Seiten rund 5000 Stichwörter, wichtige Redewendungen und Sätze zu typischen Situationen. Zahlreiche mehrfarbige Fotos und lustige Illustrationen vermitteln landeskundliche Informationen in Wort und Bild. Ein unentbehrlicher Begleiter für jedem PONS-Reisewörterbuch auch eine Compact-Cassette. PONS-Reisewörterbücher von Klett sind in jeder guten Buchhandlung erhältlich.

Englisch

Klettbuch 51861
Compact-Cassette dazu:
Klettnummer 51871

Französisch

Klettbuch 51862
Compact-Cassette dazu:
Klettnummer 51872

Italienisch

Klettbuch 51863
Compact-Cassette dazu:
Klettnummer 51873

Spanisch

Klettbuch 51864
Compact-Cassette dazu:
Klettnummer 51874

Punkt für Punkt zuverlässig